BART: a Life of A. Bartlett Giamatti

By Him & About Him

Anthony Valerio & Robert Brower

New Paperback Edition

Praise for BART:

"The book brims over with examples of Bart's eloquence. It contains, as well, quotations about Giamatti from his colleagues in both academia and baseball, and from people familiar with his life from his earliest days growing up in Holyoke, Massachusetts, where Dante *and* baseball were topics of conversation around the family dinner table. BART contains a wealth of images associated with Giamatti's life ranging from a photograph of the gas station where Holyoke men and boys gathered to listen to the Red Sox games to a sampling of Italian art works and photography associated with his scholarly pursuits...a deft and balanced selection."
--Yale Magazine

"A wonderful read."--Larry King, USA Today

"This book…is a celebration of baseball as an essential fiber of Americana. It is inspirational, thought-provoking and unique."--The Arizona Daily Star

"Exquisite and elegant."-- Yankee Magazine

Anthony Valerio is the author of six books and numerous stories and essays, including "Maglie in Paradise" from *Reaching for the Stars* (Random House). He lives in Connecticut near many active ball fields.

photo by Mathew DeGannon

Robert Brower lives in central Vermont in the hills around Montpelier. He teaches yoga when he's not following the baseball season on the radio.

White Horse Tavern. 2004. Photo by Caitlin Brower

This book is dedicated to A. Bartlett Giamatti and the Giamatti Family

To Ellen, my captain. Anthony

To Scottie, many thanks. Robert

BART was originally published in 1991 by Harcourt, Brace Jovanovich. Harvest paperback, 1993.

E-edition Copyright© Daisy H Productions LLC. 2012. Print edition Copyright© Daisy H Productions LLC 2013.

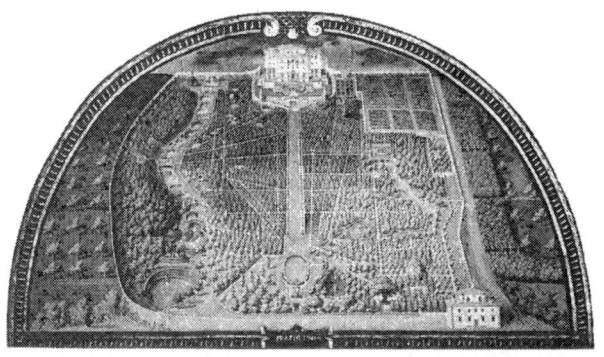

Renaissance Garden of the Villa Medici at Pratolino by Van Utens, Museum of Florence. Alinari/Art Resource

Introduction: Safe in Elysium

September 1, 1989. The tragic news came to me over the radio, National Public Radio. It was the appropriate station and medium, I would discover, because he was a very "public" man and his passion for baseball was sparked by listening to Red Sox games over the radio in the gas station of his small New England hometown. Even when he was in a ballpark, the game played "in the only place it will last," he wrote--"the enclosed green field of the mind." Often, during the making of this book, I pictured myself as a boy sitting on my father's belly of a Saturday afternoon, listening to crime shows on our radio. Bart had a way of evoking lovely memories, of taking us home.

After I heard the news, I wanted him to play more clearly in my mind. I knew only that he was commissioner of baseball, had been embroiled in a terrible dispute with one of the game's greatest players, and had been president of Yale. Premier educator and top baseball official in one lifetime--maybe the stunning disparity between the two professions had launched the man beyond my ability to understand.

I had also seen him in the stands, sitting among ordinary fans. The commissioner not sitting up in the press box, protected by glass, surrounded by other dignitaries. Odd. Provocative, too.

Immediately, I went to my university's library in search of his books. Writer to writer, teacher to teacher, fan to fan—his books would show me how his mind really worked. I was not acquainted with their titles, but the computer instructed that I could type in the author's name and the titles would follow. A process that probably would have drawn an amused smile from him--I was partially in the dark but could find my way by following the rules.

I typed, "A. Bartlett Giamatti," and the first title to appear was his very first book, *The Earthly Paradise and the Renaissance Epic.* It was published in 1966, twenty years before he became the president of the National League.

I located the book and, standing in the stacks, opened it to the first page of chapter one, entitled "Gardens and Paradises." I thought, A baseball field, at least one made of natural grass and out-of- doors, is a kind of garden--an ideal construction, an enclosed green place nourished by the sun and mild breezes and sometimes rain. And for millions of us, I thought further, a baseball field is paradise in that on such a field our favorite game is played, and this game is a reward for good living, and through watching and playing it, we experience happiness.

Everyone called him Bart, and now Bart was beginning to paint my mind green.

Green, I knew, is the color of hope, and with the hope of understanding I read the first sentence of chapter one: "The place of perfect repose and inner harmony is always remembered as a garden."

I looked away and, in the green field of my mind, took the liberty of changing only one word, the last one. Now the sentence read: "The place of perfect repose and inner harmony is always remembered as a ballpark."

Still, the link between his passions was of my creation, but I was fascinated and went on to read all his writings, and writings about him. I learned that he had carried his loves for baseball and literature throughout his life: from his childhood, when Dante and baseball were discussed at the dinner table; to his years as a university professor, when he took out time to write a prize-winning article on Tom Seaver; to his tenures as university president and baseball commissioner. He was equally eloquent when writing about both disciplines, equally intelligent and original.

Then I saw the Renaissance garden of the

Villa Medici in Florence, Italy. It is, of course, green, and I was shocked and delighted to see that it's shaped like a diamond. You begin the experience at home, the palace, and end it at home. The journey is serene, enriching. You travel along paths from one base of safety to another--from statue to statue, fountain to fountain. This book began to form, a view of Bart's life with his two passions existing side by side, as perhaps he viewed it himself. His life and work inspired vivid images and manifested profound thought-- images of his heroes and the places he loved, such as Fenway Park, his father, Martha's Vineyard, Bobby Doerr, Dante, Ted Williams. Bart loved the springtime. He loved free inquiry. He loved America. He was also a hero, an American Renaissance Man. Family, journalists, students, and colleagues in academia and in baseball, all view him from their own special angles, with the result that Bart's life emerges as a fascinating prism-- sparkling, multi-faceted, beautiful.

In the library, I guess I wanted to see him in the stands again, just another fan, leaning forward with his soft tan hat on, all attention riveted on the field.

I flipped ahead a few pages to the author's first citation of poetry, a description of the Elysian Fields, which are promised Meneláos in the fourth book of Homer's Odyssey:

The gods intend you for Elysion

with golden Rhadamanthos at the world's end,

where all existence is a dream of ease.

Snowfall is never known there, nor long frost of winter, nor torrential rain, but only mild and lulling airs from Ocean bearing refreshment for the souls of men--the West Wind always blowing.

I went home feeling slightly better. I had learned two things. The gods had intended Bart Giamatti for Elysium, and he was there.

--ANTHONY VALERIO

The Elysian Fields, Hoboken New Jersey.
National Public Library, Cooperstown, New York

Q: Would Dante have approved of your new job as president of the National League?

A: "I think Dante would have been delighted. I think Dante knew very well that the nature of paradise was and what preceded it. He would have approved of any sport whose first game in 1845 was played on something called the Elysian Fields in Hoboken, New Jersey."

--A. BARTLETT GIAMATTI
from "Dante to Doerr" *by* Nick Johnson

Radio and the Red Sox

The real activity was done with the radio--not the all-seeing, all-falsifying television-- and was the playing of the game in the only place it will last, the enclosed green field of the mind.

-A. BARTLETT GIAMATTI, "The Green Fields of the Mind"

EULOGY OVER THE RADIO

One of Bart's writings on baseball usually concluded the season of Red Sox radio broadcasts. On September 1, 1989, before the Red Sox played the Seattle Mariners, the Sox radio announcer Ken Coleman made an exception. He read the following:

It breaks your heart. It is designed to break your heart. The game begins in the spring, when everything else begins again, and it blossoms in the summer, filling the afternoons and evenings, and then as soon as the chill rains come, it stops and leaves you to face the fall alone. You count on it, rely on it to buffer the passage of time, to keep the memory of sunshine and high skies alive, and then just when the days are all twilight, when you need it most, it stops .... And summer is gone.

--A. BARTLETT GIAMATTI, "The Green Fields of the Mind"

Fenway Park, Boston
National Baseball Library, Cooperstown, New York

THE RED SOX, THE UNIVERSE

"About the only thing to do in summer was ride my bike and listen to Boston Red Sox games on the radio. I was probably seven or eight years old when my father and uncle took me to my first baseball game. I'd been listening on the radio often enough, but going to Fenway Park, I was just astonished at the whole thing."

--A. BARTLETT GIAMATTI, from "Professor Hardball" by Brenton Welling and William C. Symonds

Bobby Doerr
National Baseball Library,
Cooperstown, New York

"The Red Sox in South Hadley, the Red Sox in small New England towns, that was it, that was the big league in every sense of the word. That was the universe," he mused, now reciting the team lineup in 1952. Bobby Doerr was his hero.

("I wanted to be Bobby Doerr.") "That was the firmament, what the Lord had put out there to give one stability, coherence and purpose in life."

-A. BARTLETT GIAMATTI, from "Insight" by Cynthia Mann

Q. Why choose to be Bobby Doerr rather than Ted Williams?

A. I could imagine myself playing second base but not hitting .400. Children Imagine, adults fantasize.

--A. Bartlett Giamatti, from "He'll forever be linked with Sox" by Jack Craig

Ted Williams
National Baseball Library,
Cooperstown, New York

He [Giamatti] recalled a long ago day when a car with New Hampshire plates stopped at this particular gas station in South Hadley, near his house, and the driver got no service at all.

"He got out and stomped around and stared at us--ten or twenty men and boys, just standing there in the service bay. He thought he'd come to a place where he could get gas, but he was wrong. The purpose was to let us stand in the shade of the bay and listen to the Red Sox. It was like that all over New England then, of course. The Sox were the lingua franca."

- -ROGER ANGELL, "The Sporting Scene: Celebration," The New Yorker

Gas station, corner of Silver and College Streets, South Hadley, Massachusetts.
Robert Brower

Q. Tell me about the Boston Red Sox in High Institutional.

A. "Okay. Impelled by a high sense of their traditional mission, the central organizing force in that northeastern part of the United States-- which, of course, is not the only part of the United States but nevertheless is, for our purposes, the part we are talking about-- the Red Sox have both fallen upon hard times and, in their own terms, achieved a significant grandeur."

--EDWARD B. FISKE, "Yale's MVP Learns New Signals-- and Sends Some"

"I used to kid him about his big words."

-- Marge Schott, owner, Cincinnati Reds

BASEBALL AS NARRATIVE

Our pleasure . . . , whose origins are far more difficult to discover than are the historical roots of any sport or game, is radically tangled up with our childhood. Much of what we love later in a sport is what it recalls to us about ourselves at our earliest. And those memories, now smoothed and bending away from us in the interior of ourselves, are not simply of childhood or of a childhood game. They are memories of our best hopes. They are memories of a time when all that would be better was before us, as a hope, and the hope was fastened to a game. One hoped not so much to be the best who ever played as simply to stay in the game and ride it wherever it would go, culling its rhythms and realizing its promises. That is, I think, what it means to remember one's best hopes, and to remember them in a game, and revive them whenever one sees the game played, long after playing is over.

I was led to these thoughts by thinking on my own love of baseball, and the origins of that emotion.

-- A. BARTLETT GIAMATTI, *Take Time for Paradise*

I keep trying to remind people that there are lots of ways to love baseball. Some come to it through a love of statistics, or the smell of the glove, or just for something that their grandfather recited to them when they were very young. I keep saying: There are many routes to the game. There are many routes to the kingdom of baseball.

--A. BARTLETT GIAMATTI, from "A Gentleman and a Scholar" by Frank Deford

*Bucky Dent breaks the heart
of every Red Sox fan
UPI, Bettmann Archives*

"I was in an airport lounge, a bar in Texas, when Bucky Dent hit the homer. Of all, that memory may stick out the most. I was really dashed."

Shortly after the devastating blow, Bart wrote an essay that appeared in the Hartford Courant. It began:

"The Old Poet Spenser said, 'Nothing is sure that grows on earthly ground.'

"He had seen the flux of matters mortal, and he knew the only constant is corrosive change. He made of that knowledge a goddess, Dame Mutabilitie, and gave her sway over all things below the moon.... He thought he knew it all. He did not.

"He had never loved the Red Sox."

--from "Giamatti: a Simple Lover of Baseball" by Kevin Paul Dupont

ONCE·A·YEAR PILGRIMAGE TO FENWAY PARK

Johnny Pesky
*National Baseball Library,
Cooperstown, New York*

"I asked him," Johnny Pesky recalled," 'Mr. President, who will you be standing up for in the seventh-inning stretch?' And he said, 'I think I'll just sit down and be quiet.'

"But I knew he was leaning our way."

One of the highlights of his 1988 season, Bart said, was a stint in the Fenway Park radio booth.

"He was filling in and we hoped to get him for half an inning," said announcer Joe Castiglione. "He stayed for five."

Sox outfielder Dwight Evans: "I met him on the field last year (1988) during batting practice. Even though he was a well-educated man, he seemed like a kid around the ballpark. He was excited about being there and he asked about the finer points of the game.

"We knew that he liked us before I met him, though. This place was close to home for him."

Red Sox general manager Lou Gorman met Bart in the Fenway press box.

"He asked me about a player at Class A. I was surprised that he would be knowledgeable enough to ask about a player that low in the minors. He knew more about the player than I did. I went and looked up the guy's average and he was having a pretty good year."

--FRANK DELL'APA, "Baseball Commissioner Giamatti Dies--Red Sox Lose a Friend of Their Family"

AN OVERHEARD MOMENT

Baseball people have the keenest eyes for the telling detail I have ever known. This might be an overheard moment--one erect, white-haired old man to two peers:

"So now Tebbetts is catching in Boston, he tells me last winter, and Parnell is pitching, it's against New York, and it's a brutal day, no wind, hot, rainy, it's going to pour and they want to get the game in, and Joe Gordon splits his thumb going into second when Junior Stevens steps on his hand, he can't pivot, and now it's the eighth, tie score, and Bobby Brown comes up with two out and Bauer sitting on third and Birdie says to Ed Hurley who's got the plate, 'This is the

Doctor, Ed, this is a left-handed doctor ...' " And it goes on, extending itself by loops and symmetrical segments and reiterations just the way the game does, as if it were yesterday and not August 1949.

- -A. BARTLETT GIAMATTI, *Take Time for Paradise*

Mel Parnell
National Baseball Library,
Cooperstown, New York

To quote Edward Bennet Williams,

"He got to the end of the beginning, not the beginning of the end."

--LARRY LUCCHINO, president, Baltimore Orioles

HOME

What's home? Home is longing for when you were happy because you were younger. At least you thought you were happier.

--A. BARTLETT GIAMATTI, *from* "Front-office Fan" *by* Todd Brewster

The Giamatti family home. Silver Street, South Hadley, MA. *Robert Brower*

REMEMBRANCE OF AN OLDER BROTHER

Everything that has been written and said is true--he was a great sportsman--but he had a great love for the classics and comparative literature as well. He was president of Yale, and he was a true scholar.

He had a great passion. Whether or not you agree with his decision in the Rose case, he tried to do what was best for the game.

He intellectualized about the game and analyzed it much more than the average fan, I think.

He was the biggest fan in town. The Sox were everything.

In the heat of the moment, we might just remember him as commissioner of baseball. But this was just another chapter in the story of his life.

--DINO GIAMATTI, *from* "He Had a Great Passion" *by* Judy Van Handle

When a man is deeply rooted, then he will be "fed with heavenly sap" (Spenser): the thick, viscous light of life will swell and replenish his soul, and the armor of his body, and his self.

- -A. BARTLETT GIAMATTI, *Play of Double Senses: Spenser's* Faerie Queene

Poetry by Raphael, Vatican. Alinari/Art Resource

MIXED HERITAGE

A. Bartlett Giamatti was born in Boston on April 4, 1938. He was raised a few blocks from Mount Holyoke College, in Hadley, Massachusetts, where his father, Valentine (Yale, '32) was a professor of Romance languages and Italian literature. Before his death, the elder Giamatti recalled discussing Dante over dinner with his young son. His mother was Mary Claybaugh Walton (Smith, '35). While it is true that one grandfather for whom he is named, Angelo Giammattei (the spelling was later altered) stepped off the boat at Ellis Island about 1900 and settled in New Haven, it is also true that about the same time the other grandfather for whom he is named, Bartlett Wilson, was leaving Andover for Harvard College. Had the backgrounds of his parents been reversed, the president of Yale would be Bartlett A. Wilson, and he probably would not have been pictured recently with a laughing and voluptuously gowned Sophia Loren in newspapers across the country at a tribute given them in Washington by the National Italian-American Foundation. Nor might published profiles say that he uses his hands when he talks, which he does no more than his predecessor (Kingman Brewster).

--WILLIAM E. GEIST, "The Outspoken President of Yale"

The 200th Anniversary of South Hadley Parade held in 1953 (Dr. Giamatti would have been 15 years old at the time) *Joseph Marcotte/South Hadley Library system*

ON BEING COMPARED WITH KINGMAN BREWSTER

I envy his superb capacities to engage the world. But I am not conscious of competing with his image, of having to confront and destroy the predecessor, as Harold Bloom writes of poets. I knew my predecessors as persons and perhaps that's why they aren't public figures to me.

--A. BARTLETT GIAMATTI, "Yale's Renaissance Man" *by* William Henry III

And when it is given one to round third, a long journey seemingly over, the end in sight, then the hunger for home, the drive to rejoin one's earlier self and one's fellows, is a pressing, growing, screaming in the blood. Often the effort fails, the hunger is unsatisfied as the catcher bars fulfillment, as the umpire-father is too strong in his denial, as the impossibility of going home again is re-enacted in what is often baseball's most violent physical confrontation, swift, savage, down in the dirt, nothing availing.

- -A. BARTLETT GIAMATTI, *Take Time for Paradise*

Baseball's most violent physical confrontation. AP/ Wide World

HOME PLATE

Home plate mysteriously organizes the field as it energizes the odd patterns of squares tipped and circles incomplete. Home plate radiates a force no other spot on the field possesses, for its irregular precision, its character as an incomplete square but finished pentagram, starts the field, if you will, playing. It begins the dance of line and circle, the encounters of energy direct and oblique, of misdirection and confrontation, of boundary and freedom that is the game, before any player sets foot on the field. Home plate also has a peculiar significance, for it is the goal of both teams, the single place that in territorially based games--games about conquering--must be symbolized by two goals or goal lines or nets or baskets. In baseball, everyone wants to arrive at the same place, which is where they start

-- A. BARTLETT GIAMATTI, *Take Time for Paradise*

INSIGHT

Asked about the familial legacy, about the struggle to develop and define himself, Giamatti was clearly ill at ease during a recent and rarely granted interview at his modest office in Woodbridge Hall. He shifted in his chair, groped to find words, started and stopped sentences midway.

"Are you sure you want all this?" he asked in wonderment. "This is very personal stuff. I never do this, I never talk about all this stuff. . . .

I am a great believer in the proposition that the unexamined life is as worth living as anybody else's. I don't really think about these things a great deal."

He dismissed his dual heritage. . . as a media hook that never seemed worth the attention paid to it.

After more reflection, he said he supposed his choice of scholarship in English and Italian literature was "some sort of ethnic confluence" for him.

He was less equivocal about his father, "an enormous influence on me, and I adored him. I think I learned all my real lessons from my father," Giamatti said. "He really was the person who taught me about teaching, and by watching him, about scholarship. I saw him teach all the time, not just in the classroom. . . . He was the first person to introduce me to literature and he gave me to understand that the academic world, while it's never a perfect world . . . is one where there are real aspirations and ideals."

But "my father didn't tell me I should be an academic, nobody told me. I decided to be an academic. I don't know when or quite even why."

Mt. Holyoke must have been a profound influence, Giamatti conceded. He spent a lot of time there, "hanging out with friends," earning money after school, discovering women and unconsciously absorbing what he called the "arcane tribal mores of the academy."

Recalling childhood times, Giamatti was digging deep. And his memory, which he said is strongly tied to South Hadley where his mother still lives, was startling, especially when it came to anecdotes about baseball.

There was that afternoon in 1946 "sitting in Frankie White's father's Chevrolet in the garage listening to the World Series between the Red Sox and the Cardinals . . . Why we were in the car . . . doubtless running down the battery, is still one of those mysteries I've never quite understood. . ."

--CYNTHIA MANN, "Insight"

Enos Slaughter scoring deciding run in the 1946 World Series against the Red Sox. *AP/Wide World*

THE WORD "HOME"

Why is home plate not called fourth base? As far as I can tell it has always been thus.

And why not? Meditate upon the name. *Home* is an English word virtually impossible to translate into other tongues. No translation catches the associations, the mixture of memory and longing, the sense of security and autonomy and accessibility, the aroma of inclusiveness, of freedom from wariness, that cling to the word *home* and are absent from *house* or even *my house*. *Home* is a concept, not a place; it is a state of mind where self-definition starts; it is origins-- the mix of time and place and smell and weather wherein one first realizes one is an original, perhaps *like* others, especially those one loves, but discrete, distinct, not to be copied. Home is where one first learned to be separate and it remains in the mind as the place where reunion, if it ever were to occur, would happen.

- - A. BARTLETT GIAMATTI, *Take Time for Paradise*

The national pastime, he said, is "an oft-told tale that recommences with every pitch, with every game, with every season." Indeed, its basic motif-leaving home and struggling to return-is as ancient as Homer. "All literary romance," Dr. Giamatti once wrote, "derives from *The Odyssey* and is about rejoining."

--EDWARD B. FISKE, "Lessons"

Bust of Homer,
Capitoline Museum, Rome
Alinari/Art Resource

HOMER'S GARDEN

*To left and right, outside, he saw an orchard
close by a pale--four spacious acres planted
with trees in bloom or weighted down for picking;
pear trees, pomegranates, brilliant apples,
luscious figs, and olives ripe and dark.
Fruit never failed upon these trees: winter
and summertime they bore, for through the year
the breathing Westwind ripened all in turn—
so one pear came to prime, and then another,*

and so with apples, figs, and the vine's fruit
empurpled in the royal vineyard there.
Currants were dried at one end, on a platform
bare to the sun, beyond the vintage arbors
and vats the vintners trod; while near at hand
were new grapes barely formed as the green bloom fell,
or half-ripe clusters, faintly coloring.
After the vines came rows of vegetables
of all kinds that flourish in every season,
and through the garden plots and orchard ran
channels from one clear fountain,
while another gushed through a pipe under the courtyard entrance
to serve the house and all who came for water.
These were the gifts of heaven to Alkinoos.

The father, who gives us life, teaches us to live together. And in revealing this civilizing impulse through the father, these large, public, historically oriented poems (epics) unfold their massive subject: man's effort to impose civilization within and without himself, his desire and need to earn citizenship in a city of man or of God. So the father tells the son in the Underworld, that deep, dark place in the self where the roots of the self begin, and so the son learns to be a father, to his people, to his city, to himself.

- -A. BARTLETT GIAMATTI, *Play of Double Senses: Spenser's* Faerie Queene

PROFESSOR GIAMATTI RETIRES FROM MOUNT HOLYOKE COLLEGE

Professor Valentine Giamatti, with part of his collection of Etruscan artifacts

Courtesy Mrs. Valentine Giamatti and Mount Holyoke College Library/Archives

Prof. Valentine Giamatti... a pivotal part of the Mount Holyoke community for the past 33 years, is former chairman of the department of Italian language and literature, professor of Italian on the Alumnae Foundation and a noted authority on the poet Dante Alighieri.

A Phi Beta Kappa graduate of Yale University in 1932 where he was recipient of the Sterling Memorial Scholarship for four years, he did advanced study at the University of Perugia and, under an American Italian Exchange Fellowship, at the University of Florence. He received his Ph.D. at Harvard University in 1940. In 1948 he received a Doctorate of Letters from the University of Florence, Italy.

An expert in the works of Dante, Dr. Giamatti has assembled one the finest private collections and illustrated editions of *The Divine Comedy* in the world, dating back as far as 1481. A collector of Etruscan artifacts and Roman coins, Dr. Giamatti is a member of the American Archeological and Numismatic Societies.

Holiday postcard made by Bart's parents, Peggy and Valentine Giamatti. Courtesy Mrs. Valentine Giamatti and Mount Holyoke College Library/Archives Photo of holiday postcard Thomas Jacob

During the war years, at the request of the United States government, Dr. Giamatti taught Portuguese at Mount Holyoke. He is the author of many translations of Italian and Portuguese articles for various periodicals.

Before coming to Mount Holyoke in 1940, Dr. Giamatti, a native of New Haven, Conn., was assistant dean and instructor in Romance languages at Vermont Junior College, now Vermont College at Montpelier.

Dr. Giamatti is married to the former Mary Walton, whom he met in Florence during the summer of 1933 when she was a student at Smith College. They have three children, A. Bartlett Giamatti, who is a professor of English and former master of Ezra Stiles College at Yale and an author in his own right; Mrs. David

Ewing, who lives in Vienna, Va., where her husband is in the government service; and Dino Giamatti, former manager of the Harbor View Hotel in Edgartown and who now owns and operates the Atlantic House Hotel in Scarborough, Me. The Giamattis have seven grandchildren.

--*The Vineyard Gazette, 1973*

Three Rivers Stadium - Pittsburg, PA. National Baseball Library, Cooperstown, New York

A PARTICULAR PLACE

Bart: Baseball has another interesting characteristic--that you come to the love of it not in the abstract but through a particular place, whether that is the place you grew up or the place you end up. People say, "I love baseball," but when you press them, they say they love the Orioles, the Padres, the Yankees or the Mets. You could no more imagine moving the World Series to a third site where the weather would be excellent ...

Life: Which has been proposed...

Bart: But which is an idea whose time will never come. I am not making a negative comment about the Super Bowl, which is fine for football. But, my god, the very notion! If you had proposed that the Twins and the Cardinals were going to play the World Series in Jack Murphy

Stadium in San Diego, why the State of Missouri and the State of Minnesota would have seceded from the Union, made common cause, and declared war on the United States. And I would have been with them!

Life: So the appeal of the game is intimately wrapped up with the place where you got to know it.

Bart: And intimately wrapped up with one's youth. Baseball is very much about being young again in a harmless way. And one of its core appeals is to remind America of a time when it was young. That's why we call it a baseball park. You can call it a stadium if you want, but they were parks originally. "Park" is a Persian word and it means "paradise." If I'm quoted saying this, George Vecsey in *The New York Times* will write some crack about how Giamatti is always making up that *haiku* stuff. I don't care. You fly over a major city at night in the summer and suddenly you'll see that green oasis that reminds everybody of baseball's basic mythology: We come from a rural, simpler America. What's home? Home is longing for when you were happy because you were younger. At least you thought you were happier. It's not a game about overpowering somebody else. Home, that's what you call that thing! It's the one baseball fact that I cannot track down in all the histories that I have read. When did that pentagram where you start and where you aspire to return, when did that get called "home"? Why isn't it fourth base? What genius so defined the essence of what we're after by calling it *home* plate?

—TODD BREWSTER, "Front-office Fan"

Paradise *by Jan Brueghel, Musée des Beaux Arts, Besançon Giraudon/Art Resource*

THE WORD "PARADISE"

The word "paradise" derives from the Old Persian word *pairidaeza* formed on *pairi* (around) and *diz* (to mould, to form) which meant the royal park, enclosure, or orchard of the Persian king. Even at its origin, the word signified a specific natural place with a special (in this case, royal) character. The subsequent history of the word has two branches: it becomes Hebrew *pardes*, and it is adapted by the Greek and, through Latin, French, and Middle English, becomes our word "paradise."

The Hebrew word, *pardes*, meant a park or garden and was used only three times in the Old Testament. There it meant specific, verdant enclosures, but had no connection with what we commonly call the earthly paradise or garden in Eden of Genesis 2:8. That specific identification was to come in later commentaries, apocalyptic and rabbinical, after *pardes* had been influenced by its Greek cognate *paradeisos*.

Gardens or orchards and the garden in Eden are not, however, the only concepts transmitted by *paradeisos*. Two New Testament authors also use the Greek word and give it a third meaning. We find it in Luke and in Paul where the references to *paradeisos* are understood to mean Heaven, the celestial paradise. Thus, *paradeisos*, through Xenophon, New Testament writers, and the LXX, has three distinct meanings: a park or royal garden, the celestial paradise or Heaven, and--most important of all--the earthly paradise or garden in Eden. The intermingling in *paradeisos* of general garden-motifs with the particular spiritual attributes of the garden in Eden not only reflected ancient (Sumerian, Babylonian, and Greek) convictions about the garden as the place of bodily ease and inward harmony; it also provided a node of spiritual and aesthetic associations for generations of Christian writers who wanted to refer to the state of body and soul which once we possessed and then we lost.

--A. BARTLETT GIAMATTI, *The Earthly Paradise and the Renaissance Epic*

HOMETOWN

When baseball tryouts for the South Hadley High baseball team were held in the spring of 1951, a small, scrappy second base candidate caught coach Tom Landers' eye.

When the final cuts came for the team, the would-be second baseman, whose goal was to play for the Red Sox, didn't earn a spot on the playing roster--but Landers found a position for him, anyway.

"Oh, he played his heart out, but he just didn't have the talent necessary to make the team," said Landers. "But he was very enthusiastic and great to have around."

Thus, the coach found a place as team manager for Bart Giamatti ....

"He was an amazing person, a fun person, what we called in those days a 'hell-raiser,' " said Ray Miner, who played on the South Hadley basketball team, which Giamatti also managed. "He never played ball but always wanted to be with the athletes."

"He was a hell of an organization person," said Landers. "When I made him manager, I saw what he could do. When the players came to the game, he would have everything down pat for them—have their gloves, the balls ready. Then, when I appointed assistant managers, he had the duties down for them, 1'00. He had everything well-organized, and he was very intelligent. ... "

"He was Red Sox crazy," said Miner. "Whenever anyone mentioned the Yankees, there was a fight when Bart was around. He knew all the players, knew their batting averages, and he was all ready for that. There was a lot of spirited talk when he argued about the Yankees and the Red Sox.

"Everybody liked him," added Miner. "He hung around with everyone and mixed with everyone. I never heard anyone say anything bad about him.

"He spent more time in the showers than we did .... After we won a game, we'd look for somebody to throw in, and it wouldn't be the coach so Bart was the one we picked.

"He came back last winter to speak at a Lions' Club dinner, and this fall we were hoping to have him come back again (for an event honoring Landers). When he heard about it, he said he wouldn't miss it for the world."

--JUDY VAN HANDLE, "Hometown Stunned, Saddened"

Ballfield, South Hadley High School. Robert Brower

I grew up believing in values, and also believing we'll often fall short of realizing them. That training probably led me to baseball. The best hitters fail about 70% of the time. But that's no reason for them, or any of us, to give up.

-- A. BARTLETT GIAMATTI, *from* "Egghead at the Plate" *by* Paul Gray

The Giamatti summer home on the outskirts of Edgartown, Martha's Vineyard
Robert Benson

Harbor View Hotel, Edgartown, Martha's Vineyard, once managed by Dino Giamatti
Robert Benson

For decades, Martha's Vineyard has been the hiding place for the wealthy and powerful, a summer enclave where people with recognizable names and faces fled to relative anonymity.

Lillian Hellman, James Taylor and Carly Simon, Katherine Graham, Mike Wallace, Beverly Sills, former Senator Edward Brooke, John Belushi, former Secretary of Defense Robert

McNamara, Jacqueline Onassis, even Frank Sinatra and his then new bride Mia Farrow have come here to avoid the maddening crowd.

For island natives, a certain sense of decorum in such situations has developed over the years, a code of conduct taught to children at an early age. Celebrities dining at Vineyard restaurants were there to eat. Period.

Martha's Vineyard was not a place for autograph seekers.

In recent years, that came as a blessing to A. Bartlett Giamatti ...

It was the family home, a place where Valentine Giamatti brought his young family of two sons and a daughter and taught them to love the ocean.

It was an affair that continued through most of the Giamatti family's life. His [Bart's] brother, Dino, had once managed the Harbor View Hotel before moving to Maine, while Bart and their father went on to distinguished academic careers as Yale professors and administrators.

L'Etoile, Edgartown, Martha's Vineyard. *Leroy Dampier*

But always they returned quietly to the Vineyard, where few knew Giamatti had moved from academia into the high-octane world of major league baseball.

"He was an excellent example of the very active and distinguished people who live off-island and lead very private lives here on the Island," said Thomas Mendenhall, Yale's master of the college in the 1950s and retired president of Smith College who now lives on the Vineyard and is a family friend of the Giamattis.

"The island tends to leave these people alone. I think his circle of acquaintances was not so large down here. Although I have known Bart for many years, I might not see him more than once a summer."

Although several of his neighbors considered Giamatti "a friend," the Vineyard was primarily a place of solitude where he would rest, write and visit his favorite French restaurants, including L'Etoile.

It was there that he recently crossed paths with sportscaster Dick Schaap, informing Schaap that he had chosen the finest restaurant on the island for his meal.

It was also here that he penned portions of his books *The Earthly Paradise and the Renaissance Epic* and *Play of Double Senses: Spenser's* Faerie Queene, as well as a recent collection of his speeches and lectures during his eight-year reign as Yale president.

Just a year ago, when Giamatti was still president of the National League, Giamatti opened his home to local reporter Richard Stradling of the Vineyard Gazette .... One of the first things he noticed was that a copy of

Giamatti's collection of speeches was on his coffee table, where it had been obviously used as a coaster by more than a few members of the Giamatti family.

In typically self-deprecating humor, Giamatti told Stradling, "I hope it makes as good a book."

Ken Goldberg, sports director of WMVY radio in Vineyard Haven, also had once spoken with Giamatti ... and he, too, had only the humor of the man to remember.

"He was very kind," Goldberg said. "He sent me a note later and said he'd be happy to do anything to help me out-- except for tickets."

--RON BORGES, "Like Many, He Found Peace on the Island"

FISHING WITH BART

Jack Livingstone is filleting cod, the sacred cod, in the kitchen of the Black Dog Restaurant in Vineyard Haven. When he finishes dealing with the daily catch, he stocks his cooler with sandwiches, a few bottles of St. Pauli Girl and heads over to Edgartown to meet Bart on the dock to the ferry to Chappaquiddick. They are going fishing.

Jack lives on Chappaquiddick. He is Bart's guide. He has a four-wheeler which can negotiate the heavy sand at the Wasque Reservation beach at the far reaches of the little island and get them to the fishing ground near the bridge.

It is a warm, sunny day in mid-October. The Red Sox are in the Series. Bart has come to get away. He sets up his pole. He smokes. They listen to Ken Coleman and Ned Martin describe the game in their literate fashion. They enjoy the cool breeze coming off the ocean. Bart speaks of Bobby Doerr, while Jack, wearing his 1950s Pittsburgh Pirates cap, sees only the great Roberto Clemente, proud, defiant, stylish.

Bart is wearing khaki trousers, a windbreaker, deck shoes with no socks and, of course, his beat-up Red Sox cap. He is beginning to relax. Fishing is not a priority. He dreams of a time when he can be here regularly, drifting in the small bays on his scallop boat. He lights up another cigarette. He is in Paradise. He is in the green field of his mind.

--ROBERT BROWER, "Fishing with Bart"

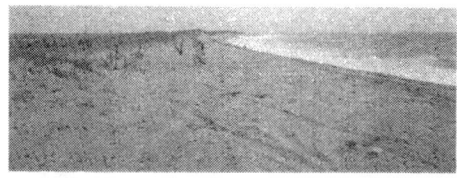

Beach at Wasque Reservation, Chappaquiddick
Caitlin Brower

Scallop boat in bay, Chappaquiddick
Caitlin Brower

Photos by Caitlin Brower

He loved the game. He wanted to be part of the team.

--TOM LANDERS, Bart's coach at South Hadley High School

Baseball and America

The ultimate purpose of the game of baseball is to bring pleasure to the American people.

--A. BARTLETT GIAMATTI, *from* "A Gentleman and a Scholar" *by* Frank Deford

Babe Ruth. *National Baseball Library, Cooperstown, New York*

BASEBALL AND THE AMERICAN CHARACTER

It would be foolish to think that all of our national experience is reflected in any single institution, even our loftiest, but it would not be wrong to claim for baseball a capacity to cherish individuality and inspire cohesion in a way which is a hallmark of our loftiest free institutions. Nor would it be misguided to think that, however vestigial the remnants of our best hopes, we can still find, if we wish to, a moment called a game, when those best hopes, those memories for the future, have life; when each of us, those who are in and those out, has a chance to gather, in a green place around home.

--A. BARTLETT GIAMATTI, "Baseball and the American Character," a speech to the Massachusetts Historical Society

Giamatti's speech is like manuscript illumination, filigrees of clauses and asides. But there's no condescension in his voice because it's armpits and balk rules being discussed and not "The Divine Comedy...." Bart Giamatti was crazy about baseball, not just as a sport of unusual symmetry and beauty but as a kind of nation-state or commonwealth with a history and a set of laws that define it and allow it to function. He thinks of baseball as a sacred American institution and of himself as one who has been entrusted to protect and administer it right down to the smallest detail.

--CHARLES SIEBERT, "Baseball's Renaissance Man"

My father's gone now, and I've come to realize that I never did ask him what baseball had meant to him——whether it had helped him to become American or feel American, the way it did in so many immigrant families.

—A. BARTLETT GIAMATTI,
*from "Celebration"
by Roger Angell,
The New Yorker*

ABOVE: *Professor Valentine Giamatti*
Courtesy Mrs. Valentine Giamatti and Mount Holyoke College Library Archives

RIGHT: *Joe DiMaggio on his way to breaking the consecutive-game hitting streak at 56*
The Sporting News

Yankee Stadium. National Baseball Library, Cooperstown, New York

THE CHRISTIAN PARADISE

The ancient image of an island, east or west, or of an Elysium; with perfect clime, perpetual springtime, a sweet west wind, fecund earth, shade and water; where under Cronos there was communal and personal harmony, bliss and ease- this image declined at times but never died. As Isidore feared, it had indeed infiltrated the Christian Allegory of consciousness and helped to form the Christian image of the earthly paradise. Because in fundamental terms of climate, food, and shelter, it represented a dream of peace for mankind, it was not dropped from Christian literature. It continued to appear in different guises for different purposes, and never failed, or fails yet, to evoke that time when the world was fresh with dew and man was happy.-

--A. BARTLETT GIAMATTI, *The Earthly Paradise and the Renaissance Epic*

Spring by Botticelli, Uffizi, Florence Alinari/Art Resource

We shouldn't be in awe of it, fall down in a heap about it. It's not paradise but it's as close as you're going to get to it in America.

--A. BARTLETT GIAMATTI, *from* "Baseball's Renaissance Man" *by* Charles Siebert

Jackie Robinson, *National Baseball Library, Cooperstown, New York*

When baseball desegregated itself in 1947 on the field, the first American insitution to do so voluntarily (before an executive order desegregated the U. S. Army, and before the Supreme Court, the public schools, and Congress passed the Civil Rights Act of 1964), baseball changed America. Baseball changed how blacks and whites felt about themselves and about each other. Late, late as it was, the arrival in the Majors of Jack Roosevelt Robinson was an extraordinary moment in American history. For the first time, a black American was on America's most privileged version of a level field. He was there as an equal because of his skill, as those whites who preceded him had been and those blacks and whites who succeeded him would be. Merit will win, it was promised by baseball. --

-A. BARTLETT GIAMATTI, *Take Time for Paradise*

Civility has to do with decency and mutual respect and, finally, with a free and ordered common life-- or civility.

--A.BARTLETT GIAMATTI, *from* "A Gentleman and a Scholar" *by* Frank Deford

He is a patriotic man who sings the national anthem at Yale football games. When a game at the Yale Bowl was close this fall, he screamed and yelled. When it was clearly lost, he amused those around with a running commentary. As the opposition team scored yet again, Mr. Giamatti spoke in grave tones to the athletic directors sitting nearby about a problem he had noticed of "this year's team being perhaps excessively deferential and overly gracious to visiting institutions." And when a fan shouted something obscene to describe Yale's play, Mr. Giamatti complimented him on "a lapidary formulation."

--WILLIAM E. GEIST, "The Outspoken President of Yale"

Carlton Fisk's 12th-inning home run ties the 1975 World Series against the Reds at three games apiece. *UPI/Bettmann Archives*

Everyone in America remembers where he was when Fisk hit his home run. My wife, Toni, and I were home in bed on Central Avenue, in New Haven, with the set on—it was after midnight, of course—and our three kids were supposed to be asleep, but, of course, they were outside, prowling around. Then they heard us yelling, and they came rushing in pretending they didn't know what was happening. We all ended up jumping up and down on the bed together.

--A. BARTLETT GIAMATTI, *from* "Celebration" *by* Roger Angell, *The New Yorker*

During the strike, Bart had been asked by the *New York Times* to write an essay for its Op-Ed page. "Call it a symptom of the plague of distrust and divisiveness that inflicts our land," he wrote, "call it the triumph of greed over the spirit of the garden. Call it what you will, the strike is utter foolishness . . . . O, Sovereign Owners and Princely players, masters of amortization, tax shelters, bonuses and deferred compensation, go back to work. You have been entrusted with the serious work of play, and your season of responsibility has come. Be at it. There is no general sympathy for either of your sides. Nor will there be. The people of America care about baseball, not your squalid little squabbles."

--CHARLES SIEBERT, "Baseball's Renaissance Man"

Bart was a close friend of mine for many, many years. He was a great person. He loved the game of baseball and in a short time made a great contribution to the game, striving for the highest possible ethical standards.

--GEORGE BUSH, former President of the United States, *The New York Times*

Teacher and Scholar

No good teacher ever wants to control the contour of another's mind. That would not be teaching; it would be a form of terrorism.

--A. BARTLETT GIAMATTI, *A Free and Ordered Space*

Young Bart talked as much about Dante as about Johnny Pesky at the family dinner table and then went to Andover and Yale. He was pledged to Scroll & Key, one of Old Eli's most secret societies; he graduated magna cum laude in 1960 and remained in New Haven to receive his doctorate, in '64. Except for a brief interlude on the faculty at Princeton, he would abide in the bosom of Yale from '56 until he resigned as the school's president in June of '86 to return to teaching. . . .

Men like Herzog ... must understand that, in many respects, Giamatti sees them first as pedagogical colleagues; he has always emphasized the point that coaches are just teachers with a different sort of classroom.

--FRANK DEFORD, "A Gentleman and a Scholar"

For being book smart, he had an awful lot of street smarts.

--WHITEY HERZOG, former St. Louis Cardinals manager, *The New York Times*

As the teams were changing sides a fan came down the aisle and introduced himself to Giamatti. "Izzy Padula," he said .... "Look I didn't want to bother you, but my cousin is Joe

Padula, who was a student of yours once, and he'd want me to say hello. He lives out in Brielle now and has a medical practice in Point Pleasant."

"Joe Padula!" Giamatti cried. "My God! Joe Padula was a student of mine for first-year Italian, back when I was an instructor at Princeton. Of *course* I remember him, but that must have been--it must have been 1964, and the class met on the second floor of East Pyne. Up the stairs and to your left. I can't believe it."

After Padula had taken his leave, carrying warm greetings to his cousin from his old teacher and invitations for him to call up when he was next in New York, I started to remind Giamatti about something, but he beat me to it, of course.

"That's *exactly* what we were talking about!" he said. "That's like an old pitcher remembering a slider he threw back in 1950. Joe Padula--isn't that amazing! I think it must have something to do with remembering times when you were really focused. It's about intensity."

- - ROGER ANGELL, "Celebration." *The New Yorker*

THE GAME'S DEEP PATTERNS

Somehow, the summer seemed to slip by faster this time. Maybe it wasn't this summer, but all the summers that, in this my fortieth summer, slipped by so fast. There comes a time when every summer will have something of autumn about it. Whatever the reason, it seemed to me that I was investing more and more in baseball, making the game do more of the work that keeps time fat and slow and lazy. I was counting on the game's deep patterns, three strikes, three outs, three times three innings, and its deepest impulse, to go out and back, to leave and return home, to set the order of the day and to organize the daylight.

- -A. BARTLETT GIAMATTI, "The Green Fields of the Mind"

Portrait of Dante, *Florence National Museum Alinari/Art Resource*

THE NUMBER NINE

And touching the reason why this number was so closely allied unto her, it may peradventure be this. According to Ptolemy, (and also to the Christian verity,) the revolving heavens are nine: and according to the common opinion among astrologers, these nine heavens together have influence over the earth. Wherefore it would appear that this number was thus allied unto her for the purpose of signifying that, at her birth, all these nine heavens were at perfect unity with each other as to their influence. This is one reason that may be brought: but more narrowly considering, and according to the infallible truth, this number was her own self: that is to say by similitude. As thus. The number three is the root of the number nine; seeing that without the interposition of any other number, being multiplied merely by itself, it produceth nine, as we manifestly perceive that three times three are nine. Thus, three being of itself the efficient of nine, and the Great Efficient of Miracles being of Himself Three Persons (to wit: the Father, the Son, and the Holy Spirit), which, being Three, are also One:-this lady was accompanied by the number nine to the end that men might clearly perceive her to be a nine, that is, a miracle, whose only root is the Holy Trinity. It may be that a more subtile person would find for this thing a reason of greater subtilty: but such is the reason that I find, and that liketh me best.

--DANTE ALIGHIERI, *A New Life*

THE AMERICAN TEACHER

I have projected a process of choice and shape as if teaching were really what the ancients and their Renaissance emulators said it was, a sculpting process, whereby the clay or stone or wax, inorganic material but malleable, could, through choices, be made to take a shape that nature never saw, a shape art supplies to the stuff the world provides. While I do not think teaching is as painless or effortless as I may have made it sound, I do believe it is essentially the ethical and aesthetic activity I propose. I do believe that it involves the making and setting of right and wrong choices in the interests of a larger, shaping process and that the deep thrill a teacher can experience comes from the combination of these activities, so that you feel what you think, do what you talk about, judge as you talk about judgment, proceed logically as you reveal logical structure, clarify as you talk about clarity, reveal as you show what nature reveals-all in the service of encouraging the student in imitation and then repetition of the process you have been summoning, all so that the student may turn himself not into you but into himself.

--A. BARTLETT GIAMATTI, *A Free and Ordered Space*

He was a warrior ... one of the greatest men I've ever been close to. He was a deep, deep man. Steeped in knowledge. Everybody else paled in comparison. He could have been anything he wanted. He could have been president. . . . Aw, Jesus. Everybody should pray for this man.

--GEORGE STEINBRENNER, *The New York Times*

Don Quichotte by *Honoré Daumier*,
Neue Pinakothek, Munich
SEF/Art Resource

...In a garden, meadow or field, poets have always felt Nature most nearly approximates the ideals of harmony, beauty, and peace which men constantly seek in one form or other. Such places, simple or ornate, realistic or idealized, are always used to symbolize some kind of satisfying experience. What the nature of that experience is depends upon the poet's personal or aesthetic needs.

--A. BARTLETT GIAMATTI, *The Earthly Paradise and the Renaissance Epic*

When Robert Yeager came to Yale in 1976 to get his doctorate in English, Giamatti was his faculty adviser and teacher of a course on Spenser.

The first class, he recalled after the banquet, was a lecture on literature, the humanities and social conscience.

Giamatti said that "in the Renaissance a poet was a man of the state as well as the page," said Yeager. He "taught the idea of service to people through letters. I had come to Yale to do what he was talking about. . . .

"He used to teach classes in shades, over his Benson and Hedges," continued Giamatti's former student. "In a gravelly voice, and in a cross between street-smart argot and the most literary language, came an understanding of the most complex Renaissance literature you can imagine .... He's a hell of a guy. .. He is a light you can follow.

"He screws up sometimes," said Yeager, "but he manages to turn his mistakes around."
- -CYNTHIA MANN, "Insight"

THE WORD "VERSE"

The poem *[Faerie Queene]* must have filled his life as he put all his humanity into it; its ideal landscapes must have become the far country of his mind, deep in the interior of his being. Certainly he saw the poet as a gardener, working the soil of the soul, a sovereign planter reordering his own inner paradise. From the beginning of his career, Spenser had understood what it meant to write a verse; that is, he knew the English word *verse* was derived from the Latin *versus*, the past participle of *vertere*, "to turn," meaning the turn of a plow, a furrow, line or row.

-- A. BARTLETT GIAMATTI, *Play of Double Senses: Spenser's* Faerie Queene

In the early 1970s, I was living in Greenwich, Connecticut, and was friendly with both Tom Seaver and Erich Segal, who were at the peaks of their different powers. Erich invited me to an Erich Segal festival at Yale-- a chance to watch the *Yellow Submarine* (which he helped write), the *Olympian* (which he wrote) and even, lucky me, the out-takes from *Love Story*. He invited me to bring Nancy and Tom Seaver along, which I did, and at some point during the evening, Erich introduced me to this guy named Giamatti, and I, in turn, introduced him to Seaver, and I had no idea at the moment that it was one of the highlights of his [Bart's] life up to that point. Giamatti later wrote that it was. I remember having a nice chat with Giamatti ... but I never suspected that he would become the commissioner of baseball, or even the president of Yale. Obviously, I had a keen reportorial eye. The last time I saw Bart Giamatti was in the summer of 1989, at a French restaurant in Vineyard Haven on Martha's Vineyard. The food was excellent. . . . We had a nice brief chat then, too. He was a good man, a literate man, an engaging man. I miss him. He was robbed, as we always said growing up in Brooklyn.

--DICK SCHAAP

TOM SEAVER'S FAREWELL

Expulsion by Masaccio.
Brancacci Chapel, Florence
Alinari/Art Resource

Tom Seaver. *National Baseball Library, Cooperstown, New York*

Near the end of his tenure as professor and the beginning of his years as Yale's president, Bart wrote a prizewinning article on the occasion of Tom Seaver's trade to the Cincinnati Reds.

Shea Stadium is not Eden, and the picture of Tom and Nancy Seaver leaving its graceless precincts in tears did not immediately remind me of the "Expulsion of Adam and Eve" in the Brancacci Chapel. And yet, absorbing the feelings generated by Seaver's departure from New York led me to the kind of inflated agitation that links Masaccio and the Mets, if only because the feelings were so outsized and anguished and intense. After all, Brad Park had gone to Boston, and Namath to Los Angeles, and Julius Erving to, if you will, Philadelphia. Clearly evil had entered the world and mortality had fixed us with its sting. If Seaver is different, and evidently he is, the reasons must be sought somewhere other than in the columns of the daily press. In fact, the reasons for Seaver's effect on us have to do with the nature of baseball, a sport that touches on what is most important in American life. Where Park, Namath and Erving are only superb at playing their sports, Seaver seems to embody his.

George Thomas Seaver almost did not become a Met. In February of 1966, the Atlanta Braves signed the University of Southern California undergraduate to a contract and assigned him to Richmond. At that point, Commissioner William Eckert stated that the signing violated the college rule. The contract was scrapped. USC, however, declared Seaver ineligible. The commissioner announced that any team, except Atlanta, matching the Richmond contract could enter a drawing for rights to negotiate. The Indians, the Phillies, and the Mets submitted to the wheel of fortune, the Mets were favored, and Seaver, signed in early April, went to Jacksonville of the International League. He was twenty-one and would spend one year in the minor leagues.

Seaver pitched .500 ball for Jacksonville, 12-12, with an earned-run average of 3.13. He would not have as weak a season again until 1974, when he would go 11-11, with an ERA of 3.20. Yet even at Jacksonville he struck out 188 batters, thus foreshadowing his extraordinary performance with the Mets, with whom, from 1968 to 1976, he would never strike out fewer than 200 batters a season--a major league record. And from the beginning Seaver pitched as much with his head as with his legs and right arm, a remarkably compact, concentrated pitcher, brilliantly blending control and speed, those twin capacities for restraint and release that are the indispensable possessions of the great artist. There is no need to rehearse the achievements of Seaver with the Mets: three Cy Young awards; Rookie of the Year with a last place ball club in 1967; the leading pitcher in the league at 25-7 (ERA 2.21) in 1969, the same year he took the Mets to their first World Series (and, in the process, reelected John Lindsay as mayor of New York--a cause for the trade no one has yet explored). In 1970 and 1971, he led the league in strikeouts (283; 289-- a league season record for right-handers) and in ERA (2.81; 1.76--which is like having an IQ of 175, though the ERA is easier to document and vastly more useful). On one April day in 1970, Seaver struck out ten Padres in a row, nineteen in all--an auto-da-fe that has never been bettered. One could go on.

The late Sixties and early Seventies were celebrated or execrated for many things besides someone being able to throw a baseball consistently at ninety-five miles per hour. These were the days of the Movement, the Counterculture, the Student Revolution; of civil rights activism, anti-war battles, student "unrest." Yippies yipped, flower children blossomed and withered. America was being greened, by grass and by rock and by people who peddled them. This was a pastoral time, and it would, like all pastorals, turn sere, but for three or four years, while Seaver was gaining control over a block of space approximately three feet high, eighteen inches wide, and sixty feet six inches long, many other of America's "young" were breaking loose. That great wave against structure and restraint--

whatever its legitimacy--begun publicly by people like Mario Savio at Berkeley in 1964, was now rolling East, catching up in its powerful eddies and its froth everyone in the country. In 1964 Tom Seaver, Californian, was moving on from Fresno City College to USC, his move East to come two years later. Here are, I think, the origins of the Seaver mystique in New York, in the young Californian who brought control, in the "youth" who came East bearing--indeed, embodying--tradition.

Most Americans do not distinguish among Californians at all, and if they do, it is certainly not with the passionate self-absorption of the natives. Yet we should, for there are real differences among them, differences far more interesting than those implied by the contrast most favored by Californians themselves, the one between the self-conscious sophisticates of San Francisco and the self-conscious zanies of Los Angeles. There are, for instance, all those Californians, North and South, who are not self-conscious at all. Such is Seaver, who is from Fresno.

Fresno--the name means "ash tree," that is, something tangible, durable; not the name of a difficult saint, with all its implications about egotism and insecurity, nor a mass of heavenly spirits, with its notions of indistinct sprawl, but "ash tree"-- Fresno is inland, about the middle of the state, the dominant city in San Joaquin Valley, that fertile scar that runs parallel to the ocean between the Coastal Ranges and the Sierra Nevada. Fresno is the kingdom sung by Saroyan-

flat, green, hot, and fertile; the land of hardworking Armenians, Chicanos, Germans; the cradle of cotton, alfalfa, raisin grapes, melons, peaches, figs, wine. Fresno is not chic, but it is secure. You do not work that hard and reap so many of the earth's goods without knowing who you are and how you got that way. This is the California Seaver came from and in many ways it accounts for his balance as a man as well as a pitcher, for his sense of self-worth and for his conviction that you work by the rules and that you are rewarded, therefore, according to the rule of merit.

All this Seaver brought East, along with his fastball and his luminous wife, Nancy. They were perceived as a couple long before this became a journalistic convenience or public relations necessity. They were Golden West, but not Gilded, nor long-haired, nor "political," nor opinionated. They were attractive, articulate, photogenic. He was Tom Terrific, the nickname a tribute to his all-American quality, a recognition, ironic but affectionate, that only in comic strips and myth did characters like Seaver exist. I have no idea what opinions Seaver held then on race, politics, war, marijuana, and the other ERA, but whatever they were, or are, they are beside the point. The point is the way Seaver was perceived as clean-cut, larger than life, a fastballer, "straight," all at a time when many young people, getting lots of newspaper coverage, were none of the above. And then there was something else, a quality he exuded.

I encountered this quality the only time I ever met Seaver. One evening in the winter of 1971 I spent several hours with the Seavers and their friends and neighbors the Schaaps . . . in the apartment of Erich Segal, then at the height of his fame as the author of *Love Story*. The talk was light, easy, and bright, and was produced almost entirely by the Schaaps, Nancy Seaver, and Segal. Because I was about the only member of the gathering who was a household name only in my own household, I was content to listen, and to watch Seaver. He sat somewhat apart, not, I thought, by design, not, surely, because he was aloof, but because it seemed natural to him. He was watchful, though in no sense wary, and had that attitude I have seen in the finest athletes and actors (similar breeds), of being relaxed but not in repose, the body being completely at ease but, because of thousands of hours of practice, always poised, ready at any instant to gather itself together and move. Candid in his gaze, there was a formality in his manner, a gravity, something autumnal in the man who played hard all summer. He sat as other men who work with their hands sit, the hands clasped chest high or folded in front of him, often in motion, omnipresent hands that, like favored children, are the objects of constant if unconscious attention and repositories of complete confidence.

Seaver had, to be brief, *dignitas*, all the more for never thinking for a moment that he had it at all. A dignity that manifested itself in an air of utter self-possession without any self-regard; it was a quality born of a radical equilibrium,

Seaver could never be off balance because he knew what he was doing and why it was valuable. He contrasted completely with the part of the country he was known to come from and with the larger society that he was seen as surrounded by. With consummate effortlessness, his was the talent that summed up baseball tradition; his was the respect for the rules that embodied baseball's craving for law; his was the personality, intensely competitive, basically decent, with the artisan's dignity, that amidst the brave but feckless Mets, in a boom time of leisure soured by divisions and drugs, seemed to recall a cluster of virtues seemingly no longer valued.

And Seaver held up. His character proved as durable and strong as his arm. He was authentic; neither a goody-two shoes nor a flash in the pan, he matured into the best pitcher in baseball. Character and talent on this scale equaled a unique charisma. He was a national symbol, nowhere more honored than in New York, and in New York never more loved than by the guy who seemed in every other respect Seaver's antithesis, the guy who would never give a sucker an even break, who knew how corrupt they all were, who knew it was who you knew that counted, who knew how rotten it all really was-- this guy loved Seaver because Seaver was a beautiful pitcher, a working guy who got rewarded; Seaver was someone who went by the rules and made it; Seaver carried the whole lousy team, God love 'em, on his back, and never shot his mouth off, and never gave in, and did it right.

The guy loved Seaver because Seaver did not have to be streetwise.

In bars in Queens, in clubs in the Bronx, in living rooms in front of Channel Nine in Suffolk and Nassau, out on Staten Island, everywhere, but particularly in the tattered reaches of Shea Stadium, they loved him for many things, but above all because he never thought he had to throw at anybody's head. From the Columbia riots to the brink of fiscal disaster, there was someone in New York who did not throw at anybody. They loved it in him, and in that act sought for it in themselves.

None of this reasoning, if such it is, would appeal to the dominant New York baseball writers, who have used the Seaver trade as a *casus belli*; nor to M. (for, I think, Moralistic) Donald

Grant, chairman of the board of the Mets, who would quickly tell us that Seaver wanted too much money, meaning by that something he would never say aloud but would certainly formulate within himself- -that Tom wanted too much. Tom wanted, somehow, to cross the line between employee and equal, hired hand and golf partner, "boy" and man. What M. Donald Grant could not abide- -after all, could he, Grant, ever become a Payson? Of course not. Everything is ordered. Doesn't anyone understand anything anymore?--Tom Seaver thought was his due. He believed in the rules, in this game governed by law; if you were the best pitcher in baseball, you ought to get the best salary of any pitcher in baseball; and money--yes, money-- ought to be spent so baseball's best pitcher would not have to work on baseball's worst hitting team.

Of course Tom Seaver wanted money, and wanted money spent; he wanted it for itself, but he wanted it because, finally, Tom Seaver felt about the Mets the way the guy from Astoria felt about Seaver--he loved them for what they stood for and he wanted merit rewarded and quality improved. The irony is that Tom Seaver had in abundance precisely the quality that M. Donald Grant thinks he values most--institutional loyalty, the capacity to be faithful to an idea as well as to individuals. Grant ought to have seen that in Seaver; after all, the man worked for the Mets for eleven years. Grant ought to have had the wit to see a more spacious, generous version of what he prizes so highly in himself. Certainly the guy who had watched Seaver all those years knew it, knew Seaver was holding out for something, a principle that made sense in one who played baseball but that grew from somewhere within him untouched by baseball, from a conviction about what a man has earned and what is due him and what is right. The fan understood this and was devastated when his understanding, and Seaver's principle, were not honored. The anguish surrounding Seaver's departure stemmed from the realization that the chairman of the board and certain newspaper columnists thought that money was more important than loyalty, and the fury stemmed from the realization that the chairman and certain writers thought everybody else agreed with them, or ought to agree with them.

On June 16, the day after Seaver was exiled to Cincinnati by way of Montreal, a sheet was hung from a railing at Shea bearing the following legend:

I WAS A BELIEVER BUT NOW WE'VE LOST SEAVER.

I construe that text, and particularly its telling rhyme, to mean not that the author has lost faith in Seaver but that the author has lost faith in the Mets' ability to understand a simple, crucial fact: that among all the men who play baseball there is, very occasionally, a man of such qualities of heart and mind and body that he transcends even the great and glorious game, and that such a man is to be cherished, not sold.

- - A. BARTLETT GIAMATTI, "Tom Seaver's Farewell: There Is No Joy in Gotham"

Shea Stadium
National Baseball Library,
Cooperstown, New York

RESTRAINT AND RELEASE

The Barbieri Races *by Gericault, Louvre, Paris.*
Giraudon / Art Resource

The geometry of baseball is constantly working against action, containing it and releasing it. There's a tremendous counterpoint between energy and order. Nothing is more orderly and geometrically precise than baseball.

--A. BARTLETT GIAMATTI, *from* "A Gentleman and a Scholar" *by* Frank Deford

Near the middle of the third *Georgic*, Virgil offers images of the power of sexual passion. One of the most striking is the horse whose whole body trembles at the familiar scent:

No longer now can the rider's rein or the cruel lash stay his course,
nor rocks and hollow cliffs, nay, nor opposing rivers,
that tear up mountains and hurl them down the wave.

The unchecked horse is the very principle of release, more powerful even than Nature at her most elemental. Because no curb can control him, he is Nature become unnatural, potency turned monstrous, as is made clear later, in the lines on the frenzied mares and their mysterious droppings--the "hippomanes," or horse madness, favored by witches... Yet, though these images of fertility run riot, the poet is able to establish images of restraint and instances of his own control. The figure of the unchecked horse allows Virgil to show how, like the farmer, he must impose limits in order to foster growth--else without art, Nature will die of her unchecked impulse. Restraint and release, and all they mean for each other, are the essence of the image, as well as of the *Georgics*.

--A. BARTLETT GIAMATTI, *Exile and Change in Renaissance Literature* (Yale University Press © 1984 by Yale University)

Through Bart's lectures on the *Inferno* and *The Faerie Queene*, he made integrity, justice, honor and fair play come alive on the page. He taught these virtues with an articulate, often theatric, Mediterranean passion, his voice at once booming and forceful, then mellifluous and soothing. He read Dante's original Italian as a maestro reads music--with love.

--W. DEWOLF FULTON , former graduate student of Bart's at the Breadloaf School of English

There are few who could say with certainty that *Orlando Furioso* is the Renaissance epic poem and "Zeke" Zarilla the right fielder of the 1952 Boston Red Sox, and not the other way around.

--WILLIAM E. GEIST, "The Outspoken President of Yale"

University President

All I ever wanted to be president of was the American League.
--A. BARTLETT GIAMATTI

Are you the man on the white horse the university had been awaiting to solve its problems?

"No. I drive a yellow Volkswagen."

--WILLIAM E. GEIST, "The Outspoken President of Yale"

"A human being as president of a university--my God, what will that be like?" quipped a colleague when Dr. Giamatti was selected by Yale's sixteen-member governing corporation.

--ROBERT D. MCFADDEN, "Giamatti, Scholar and Baseball Chief, Dies at 51"

Of course there are those who learn after the first few times. They grow out of sports. And there are others who were born with the wisdom to know that nothing lasts. These are the truly tough amongst us, the ones who can live without illusion, or without even the hope of illusion. I am not that grown up or that up-to-date. I am a simpler creature, tied to more primitive patterns and cycles. I need to think something lasts forever, and it might as well be that state of being that is a game; it might as well be that, in a green field, in the sun.

- -A. BARTLETT GIAMATTI, "The Green Fields of the Mind"

In line at a cafeteria-style restaurant in New Haven, Mr. Giamatti explained his own view of Yale's mission in animated fashion: "Not to make one technically or professionally proficient, but to instill some sense of the love of learning for its own sake, some capacity to analyze any issue as it comes along, the capacity to think and to express the results of one's thinking clearly, regardless of what the subject matter might be."

So transfixed was the woman behind the counter with this eruption that she poured almost the entire contents of a coffee pot into a single cup.

--WILLIAM E. GEIST, "The Outspoken President of Yale"

RUMINATIONS ON UNIVERSITY PRESIDENCY

Being president of a university is no way for an adult to make a living. Which is why so few adults actually attempt to do it. It is to hold a mid-nineteenth-century ecclesiastical position on top of a late-twentieth-century corporation. But there are those lucid moments, those crystalline experiences, those Joycean epiphanies, that reveal the numinous beyond and lay bare the essence of it all. I have had those moments. They were all moments of profound and brilliant failure but string those glistening moments of defeat into a strand and you have the pearls of an administrative career.

In the six months between being named president of Yale University in December of 1977 and taking office in July of 1978, I had ample opportunity to receive advice. I listened to many people. I learned about the corporate world. I learned that because the corporate world is interested only in quarterly results, it talks a great deal about long-range planning. It was clear to me that Yale needed some of that, too. We needed a corporate strategy; we needed a policy. I, of course, had no policies. I had a mortgage and one suit, but no policies. I cast about. I solicited data and forecasts and projections and models. I did comparative studies, longitudinal studies; I made a flowchart and convened a task force. I hired and fired management consultants. I went in search of a policy. What was it that Yale needed most, wanted most, and would most contribute to solving our deficit, enhancing our quality, and making me a Manager?

One night in early April 1978, crouched in my garage, as I was trying to memorize the Trustees' names, particularly the ones I had met, it came to me, and I wrote, right there, between the lawnmower and the snow tires, a memo. On July 1, 1978, my first day in office, I issued this memo to an absent and indifferent University. It read, "To the members of the University Community: In order to repair what Milton called the ruin of our grandparents, I wish to announce that henceforth, as a matter of University policy, evil is abolished and paradise is restored. I trust all of us will do whatever possible to achieve this policy objective."

The reaction was quite something.

Four young members of the faculty in Comparative Literature wrote an open letter to the *New York Review of Books* proving that Milton was talking not about evil in *Paradise Lost* but about irony and the patriarchal abuse of power. A junior in Yale College, spending the summer doing a leveraged buyout of a Tastee-Freez in Easthampton, wrote me a gracious letter. She recognized the pressure one was under to have a business plan, but she hoped that I would wait until she had graduated before changing things very much. An alumnus in New York, on Yale Club stationery, wondered why the hell we always had to get so far out in front.

In September, the *Yale Daily News* wrote the first editorial about my memo. Its opening sentences were these:

"Giamatti's administration is off to a miserable start. Rather than giving us control over our lives, or at least addressing concerns of students such as the crying need for a student center so we can make friends or any of the myriad of other injustices that riddle the fabric of the quality of life here, the new administration is insensitive and repressive and the future bodes awful."

Though one of the best-written of the *News* editorials, it was, be fair, also the first.

--A. BARTLETT GIAMATTI, *A Free and Ordered Space*

I never did have a big plan. I just wanted to be a professor of English--at Yale. I hoped--and when I accomplished that, it was almost immediately taken away from me.

--A. BARTLETT GIAMATTI,
From "A Gentleman and a Scholar" *by* Frank Deford

HORACE'S PARADISE

Let us seek the Fields, the Happy Fields, and the Islands of the Blest.
Jupiter set apart these shores for a righteous folk, ever since with bronze he dimmed the lustre of the Golden Age.

With bronze and then with iron did he harden the ages, from which a happy escape is offered to the righteous, if my prophecy is heeded.

THE OUTSPOKEN PRESIDENT OF YALE

"Life for our family changed dramatically when I became president," says Mr. Giamatti.

He laments the loss of time with his wife, the former Toni Smith, whom he met at Yale and married in 1960, and their three children-- Marcus, Elena, and Paul.

After his appointment as president, Mr. Giamatti and his family moved from a modest gray frame home in the Westville section of New Haven into the imposing servant-staffed President's House, on Hillhouse Avenue, which Charles Dickens is said to have described as the most beautiful street in America. "We live upstairs in a public building," Mr. Giamatti says, strolling through the well-appointed living room and across an Oriental carpet so vast one half expects to find free-throw circles in its intricate design. He seems unfazed by this and other trappings provided as a backdrop for official entertaining.

A characteristic of Mr. Giamatti's that a friend worried might prove debilitating in a job where every act seems certain to offend one of the dozens of his constituencies is "his being very sensitive, thin-skinned." While others also mention this trait, those close to him believe he has since developed sufficient calluses to keep from being "stung to death by gnats."

It is Mr. Giamatti's speeches that have brought praise and condemnation raining down upon him and stamped him "the outspoken president of Yale." They have stirred controversy on subjects ranging from football recruiting to the Moral Majority…

--WILLIAM E. GEIST, "The Outspoken President of Yale"

"As a sign of its commitment to athletics, Yale will treat athletics according to the same central educational values and with the same desire for excellence that it brings to other essential parts [of the university].... Let it go forth that there is a strong spirit at Yale, a strong spirit compounded of respect for the glories of mind and body striving in harmony."

Notwithstanding these noble sentiments, the speech irritated a good many alumni because Giamatti also suggested that college athletics were getting out of whack, even in the Ivy League. Says Giamatti, "I was supposed to have called for our athletics to be de-emphasized, a word I never used, any more than I would employ that vile phrase 'student-athlete.'" Indeed, those old Bulldogs who were so upset by their president's words might reread this part of the speech:

"I don't want there to be any doubt about what I believe. I think that winning is important. Winning has a joy and discrete purity to it that cannot be replaced by anything else. Winning is important to any man's or woman's sense of satisfaction and well-being. Winning is not everything, but it is something powerful, indeed beautiful, in itself, something as necessary to the strong spirit as striving is necessary to the healthy character.

THE MORAL MAJORITY

I do not fear that these peddlers of coercion will eventually triumph. The American people are too decent, too generous, too practical about their principles, to put up with the absolutism of these "majorities" for very long. Nor do I think that when these groups have finally gone back into their burrows of frustration and anger, to lie seething until the next time, the values they now pervert will be done lasting harm. For what they claim they espouse--love of country, a regard for the sanctity of life and the importance of the family, a belief in high standards of personal conduct, a conviction that we derive our values from a transcendent being, a desire to assert that free enterprise is better than state ownership or state control--are not evil or pernicious beliefs. Quite the contrary. They are the kernels of beliefs held dear, in various ways, by me and by millions of other Americans. You should not scorn these ideas simply because some extremists claim, whether sincerely or hypocritically, to have captured these beliefs for themselves. The point is, the rest of us hold to ideas of family, country, belief in God, *in different ways.* The right to differ, and to see things differently, is our concern.

--A. BARTLETT GIAMATTI, *A Free and Ordered Space*

THE WORD "ATHLETE"

As is customary, we can discover how we think about ourselves by looking at how we speak about ourselves. Two words of ancient Greek, *athlon* and *athlos*, shape a third, *athletes*. *Athlos* meant a contest; *athlon*, a prize won in a contest, and they provide us with *athletes*, an individual competing for a prize in the public games. Here in small compass is much of the ancient Greek world. Life and all that is valuable is seen as a contest. Struggle and contention lie at the core of everything, and one must devote all one's being to winning. If one wins, there is a prize, a tangible mark of triumph in the endless competition. Merit, skill, capacity-call it what you will-must be tested, and if victorious, rewarded.

No part of Greek life was immune to this view of competition or to the possibility of triumph. If you won a footrace or chariot race, you could ask Pindar to immortalize your achievement in an ode; if you were Aeschylus or Sophocles or Euripedes, and you won the annual three-day contest for dramatists in Athens, you gained a prize. By the fifth century B. C. , what we would call the realms of the athletic and the artistic were not separate in the intensity of competition or in the assumption that reward would follow victory or in the importance placed on the activities by the culture. The athlete and the artist lived in the same world and did the same thing: they both asserted the spirit in order to thrust the individual beyond time and achieve something permanent.

--A. BARTLETT GIAMATTI, "Yale and Athletics" *A Free and Ordered Space*

LESSONS

Dr. Giamatti threw himself into the task of soothing alumni and soliciting contributions for unglamorous purposes. "Call me Bart the Refurbisher," he told a reporter on his retirement from Yale in 1985. "I've spent $20 million on deferred maintenance and will only be remembered by people who like to go through steam tunnels. If my name goes on anything, it will be the Giamatti Memorial Wiring System."

His seven years at Yale took a toll on him physically. He never learned to leave work at the office. Things were not helped by his heavy smoking and the strike by clerical workers, which he appeared to view as an affront to his concept of academic community. His hair grayed, his step lost its bounce. Friends worried out loud about his health.

Bart Giamatti brought passion to whatever he felt called to do. He cared about Yale and baseball and scholarship and the English language, and pursued all of these with gusto, dignity, eloquence and wit. He disregarded the price that a private person-especially one whose first instincts lie in "stalking and grabbing" an idea-pays for a public life.
--EDWARD B. FISKE, "Lessons"

I looked on him as my captain, in the sense in which the American poet uses this term.

His balance between the intellectual and the practical was not, as in most cases, the result of ageing and mellowing. Rather, it was the product--one surmised--of a strenuous search which called on all the resources of his electric vitality. A Renaissance scholar who turns college president is a fit subject for a curricular chronicle in a reassuring and stately mode. But a man who does this with the nobility, vivaciousness and torment which help explain those twisted homages that were the personal attacks on him during the strike at Yale, a man who then goes out of the university and into the world of baseball-- such a man is a fit subject for a novel, for only a narrative can address the cluster of tensions and desires that lie behind these transitions.

I felt for him a trace of that mixture of close affection, distant admiration and rebelliousness that one feels (what matters the crude biological fact that we were contemporaries?) for one's father.

On a fall day in the airport limousine, still dazed by the oceanic flight, I saw the fragment of a screaming title in the newspaper rolled up beside the driver.

The minutes that intervened between this sight and the reluctant decision to spread open the paper and take in the death notice were the beginning of that wisdom which is simply another name for wonderment- wonder at how death seems at times to take revenge on the intensification of life, leaving us behind in that kind of slightly abject acceptance of ourselves that is the other side of wisdom.

--PAOLO VALESIO, author and professor of Italian.

"He even felt he had to respond to all the mail," says George May, a professor of French who served as Giamatti's provost for two years, "and that in itself is suicidal."

One day, a letter arrived from a seventh grader, Kempton Dunn, who wanted to know why Yale's president thought it was important to study the dead language of Latin.

Bart wrote: "We study Latin because without it we cannot know our history and our heritage. And without that knowledge, we cannot know ourselves. *Nosce teipsum* (know thyself), brave Dunn."

--FRANK DEFORD, "A Gentleman and a Scholar"

Marvin Miller, former head of the Major League Baseball Players Association (in response to Bart's essay in the New

York Times, *which concluded, "The people of America care about baseball, not your squalid little squabbles":*

"I sent him a letter," recalls Miller, who retired from the association in 1983, "and pointed out that I thought it was anti-union and that he didn't sound much different than an uninformed, bigoted fan. He wrote me a letter back defending himself, arguing this and that. So I wrote a second letter in which I objected to his line that anybody can resolve a dispute, that strikes are foolish, that it's simple to sit down and work things out. Some time later, he found himself with a strike on his hands (by Yale's clerical workers) and I'm very proud of the fact that I restrained myself from writing him a letter quoting his own lines about how it's stupid to have these disputes, and let's get back to the business of education."

--CHARLES SIEBERT, "Baseball's Renaissance Man"

"What he could have done in the future is, of course, a matter of speculation," said Haywood Sullivan, chief executive officer of the Boston Red Sox. "But he would have made a mark. In fact, he already had, and he'd done it with his intelligence, his character and his integrity."

-- JOE SEXTON, "Peers Reflect on the Loss of Giamatti"

Hercules and the Centaur by Giovanni Bologna, Loggia dei Lanzi, Florence Alinari/Art Resource

YALE'S MVP LEARNS NEW SIGNALS-- AND SENDS SOME

President Giamatti dined at Mory's with Edward B. Fiske, education editor of The New York Times, and reflected on the changes in his life, on presidential perceptions and even on presidential language--a unique dialect of

English. Following are excerpts from that conversation.

Q. Robert Hutchins once described a university as a collection of independent departments linked by a common heating system. Have you found that accurate?

A. No. A university ought to be an ecosystem, where everything is dependent on everything else. A true university is much more like a swamp.

Q. What's it like to go from being a faculty member to managing an ecosystem?

A. You go from a world in which you are in control of what you are doing-- your classroom or your research--to a situation in which you must not think that you are ever going to finish anything. When you teach, there is the satisfaction of seeing a face light up or sensing progress across a semester. When you're teaching Shakespeare, you know that you're not doing it alone--you're doing it with the students and with everyone from Coleridge on up who has dealt with Hamlet. But you've got the reins. As an administrator you maintain other people's capacity to give shape and contour. That's a very large change.

Q. How do you make that kind of adjustment?

A. You try to keep two things in mind. The first is your basic training, which is essentially pedagogical. You try to react to situations as if they were--though they aren't--teaching situations. The second is the essential core of values and traditions and hopes that the place has. You have to embody this, whether you're talking to a crowd outside your home or a single human being in your office or an alumnus in city X asking you about coeducational bathrooms. The danger, of course, is that people like me begin to think that they are the institution-as opposed to being one of the symbolic containers of these values. You become a public person. And yet you don't sit around saying, "I am a public person." You simply lose yourself.

Q. Do you ever have a sense that you're winging it?

A. Of course. That's part of the excitement. But that's also like teaching. When you speak, for instance, there are always people in your audience who know vastly more about a given issue than you do. The incident that will always stick in my mind was one night at the Mayflower Hotel in Washington. About 850 people came out to hear me talk, and about 70 percent of them must have been lawyers. The first question was, "What do you think about the Bakke decision?" and there's Potter Stewart sitting in the audience. Well, you've got to look at yourself and giggle a touch.

Q. How did you handle it?

A. I cast the answer in the subjunctive. "Were one to adopt a reasonable set of . . ." and so forth. You try to be responsive without pretending either that you're an expert or that anyone knows finally what the Bakke decision really means anyway.

THE TALK-SHOW PHENOMENON

Q. What's the difference between the scholarly and the administrative mentality?

A. As an administrator you can retain a wide range of facts because you listen to bright people and talk about them all day. But you can't drop down. You can't go very deep on a lot of things. It's the talk-show phenomenon.

I was trained to be someone who, if asked a question about something he knew about and pushed hard enough, would be able to be discursive and follow it out and see where it was going to go. Now I don't have the luxury or the leisure to be able to sit for a long time and to sink down. I fight that in myself. I fight that necessity.

Q. What do you miss most about not being a professor?

A. What I really miss--aside from time with my family, which is the worst part-- is that wonderful leisurely capacity, which was very intense, of going to the library with a problem and beginning to track it down. To hunt it, stalk it wherever it took you and then go grab it.

This kind of leisurely wandering with a purpose takes time. It can take a day, or it can take a week. I remember in the case of one essay I was writing it took about a year. But you finally get to the point where you've got the creature. Other people may have captured more handsome specimens of the thing, but that's not the issue. It's finally working it through.

Q. What took you a year to stalk?

A. I was writing on Proteus. I was stalking what people in the Renaissance thought of themselves when they kept comparing themselves to Proteus the shape-changer. What did it mean when the

Renaissance kept talking about one's ability to take a new shape? It took a long time for me to read enough, accumulate all those references and run them all back through the texts they were in to see what they really meant in Shakespeare or Erasmus or Ariosto. But eventually I began to get a shape to that set of shapes. My obsession with shapes is longstanding. And it took a long time.

Q. Do you still have time to write?

A. What you give up is the time to write the things that mean the most to you personally. What you do is find the time to write the things that mean the most to you institutionally.

Q. What has becoming president done to your language?

A. In terms of spoken language, it has made me more cautious and less colorful. What it does to one's written prose is something quite awful. You don't write anything any more except in a style that I suppose you might call High Institutional.

Q. What's that?

A. It's basic college-president prose that is not necessarily bland but takes the high road rhetorically.

Q. I don't know what that is.

A. Working journalists don't. It is prose that is meant to be noncontroversial. It is prose that eschews the rhetorical quirks that we end up identifying as style. You don't write with much flair. Syntactically it's all terribly qualified. Subordinate clauses and independent clauses match each other up, and there is a lot of parallelism of tenses and participles balancing off. It is always "this and that" because there are so many things to juggle.

Luis Tiant. *UPI/Bettmann Archives*

Q. As president of Yale, what did you think about Luis Tiant leaving the Red Sox and signing with the Yankees?

A. Luis Tiant, on the one hand, knowing full well the ravages of time--as, of course, we all as human beings come to know them--but on the other hand, ever mindful of the need to advance the human spirit, played the part of a traitor and left Boston for the asphalt pastures of New York.

Q. "Asphalt pastures?"

A. You see, that's where you save yourself from the rest of that sentence. You give them "asphalt pastures," and the only thing they get out of it is asphalt pastures because those who are listening are so tired of this prose that they look for any kind of help.

Q. Are you conscious about falling into this kind of language?

A. I feel it worst when I deal in triads. Proust said that Baudelaire always used three adjectives, and I can feel something like that happening. "Mission, purpose and hope." "Faculty, students and staff." You feel a triad taking over. Everything is a trinity.

Q. Any other signs of creeping High Institutional?

A. Yes. You feel yourself beginning to jiggle along in iambic pentameter. I gave a talk the other night in New York, and a man, a really close friend, came up to me and said, "You've got to watch out. You're doing it in iambs." I thought he meant "I am's."

Q. An "I ambiguity?"

A. An "I ambiguity." A triple pun. When you begin to do iambic pentameter, you're also beginning to say "I am the king." And that's what you want to avoid. You want to avoid the regular thump of the language, the regular thump of "I am the sovereign. I will cure your scrofula."

Q. Since you're into iambic pentameter, will you be giving a commencement address called Paradise Lost?

A. College presidents are in the business of talking about Paradise Regained. We all know that we've lost paradise, but it's coming back any moment. Probably tomorrow. If not tomorrow, then certainly by 1990 when the demographic curve goes back up.

Now can I go home?

Q. Do you have a prediction on the Red Sox?

A. The Red Sox will acquit themselves with their customary nobility and sense of despair.

Q. Is that High Institutional?

A. No, that's from the heart. They'll do very well, and paradise will always remain just beyond us.

-- EDWARD B. FISKE, "Yale's MVP Learns New Signals--and Sends Some"

As a professor, he railed against pass-fail courses and led an unsuccessful revolt against a "relevant" seminars program in the residential colleges that, for example, brought in Howard Cosell to lecture on sports. Mr. Giamatti advocated allocating those funds for an intensive writing program for freshmen.

--WILLIAM E. GEIST, "The Outspoken President of Yale"

He gave of himself magnificently as teacher, scholar and leader.

--BENNO C. SCHMIDT, former president of Yale, *from* "Giamatti, Scholar and Baseball Chief, Dies at 51" *by* Robert D. McFadden

President of the National League

Baseball's "choice of a bearded Ivy League scholar-prexy as the twelfth president of the senior circuit was a startler unmatched in the pastime since Al Weis's home run for the Mets in the fifth game of the 1969 World Series."

-- ROGER ANGELL

Today, Giamatti has attained a rare position-- that of administrator of his own refuge.

--CHARLES SEIBERT, "Baseball's Renaissance Man"

Illustration by Sebastiana Ricci for Orlando Furioso, *Museo Brukenthal, Romania. Alinari/Art Resource*

Giamatti gets slightly cagey when he is asked why he was sought out by the National League owners in the first place. "I don't know. I never asked. I haven't dared lest people think it through again." He cites the episode from *Orlando Furioso* by Ludovico Ariosto in which a knight is given a magic cup and told that if he drinks out of it he will know everything about his beloved's past. "He very wisely decides not to drink," says Giamatti. "Why ask? Take reality as it comes."

--CHARLES SIEBERT, "Baseball's Renaissance Man"

ARIOSTO

Ariosto seems to be aware of everything, and that is the level upon which his much celebrated irony operates. Ariosto is constantly examining experience with experience; he is constantly turning attitudes, statements, codes, visions--in short, appearances, words--back upon themselves. The old chivalric code is always being examined by its behavior under stress and the limitations of chivalry in the modern day emerge as one of the themes of the poem. Love as an ideal of physical or spiritual existence is repeatedly subjected to scrutiny, and countless episodes reveal its shortcomings, delusions, absurdities. Things never are what they seem. There is too much going on, impinging, underlying, ever to allow one man's set of standards or absolutes the final say. Between what seems and what is, lies either the sane, middle path, open to a few, or the bitter road of futility and delusion, taken by most. And yet--perhaps both ways are finally the same; perhaps the road to sense is also the same as the path to non-sense. Perhaps the only answer or standard or guide to life is that there is no answer, guide, or standard. What is finally most important is that man be tolerant--that is, that man be forever aware of the many possibilities, contingencies, new realities which can exist under a single, simple-seeming guise.

--A. BARTLETT GIAMATTI, *The Earthly Paradise and the Renaissance Epic*

IN A WHOLE DIFFERENT LEAGUE NOW

"The toughest thing about this job is that I will no longer be able to root for the Red Sox."

--A. BARTLETT GIAMATTI

"Smokey Joe' Wood, *National Baseball Library, Cooperstown, New York*

New National League president A. Bartlett Giamatti's kitchen was hotter than usual on Friday afternoon, the day before the first game of the ['86] World Series. "My older son calls me Benedict Arnold," said Giamatti, "and my younger son looks at me and says, 'One should always put honor before duty.' My pragmatist daughter in the middle is planning to wear her Mets cap to the game."

The vilification Giamatti received from his sons has everything to do with hats. For the first game itself, played in New England-ish 51 degree temperatures, the NL president-elect's elegant brown suede was an easy selection. More onerous was the decision of the former president of Yale to wear the hat of his new office. For years Giamatti enjoyed a reputation as academe's biggest Red Sox fan, and now as the NL's leader, he must root for his league's representative in the World Series. Says Giamatti, "It's terribly difficult, and I didn't expect to be presented with what people perceive as a dilemma. But I'm wholeheartedly behind the Mets, as I would have been wholeheartedly behind the Astros."

While his children railed at him, the 48-year-old Giamatti considered his position. Growing up in Massachusetts he had listened faithfully to radio broadcasts from Fenway Park. As president of Yale he drove around New Haven in a battered yellow Volkswagen with a frayed Red Sox bumper sticker on the rear. Why, just beyond the kitchen, in his study, sits a Red

Sox hat given to Giamatti by the late Smokey Joe Wood, the star pitcher of the 1912 World Series champions and a habitué of Yale games.

But now Giamatti must abandon the hat, abandon Smokey Joe, abandon his sons and root for the Mets. Never mind that ex-Yalie Ron Darling would be pitching for the New Yorkers. This was treason. Or was it?

"You never forget the first girl you fall in love with," says Giamatti. "But passions change and mature." He cherishes baseball as an art, so quite naturally he explains his fresh loyalties in aesthetic terms. "You might come to love art, portraiture through Velazquez. And then you discover Ingres and become a devotee of his work. But what you really love is portraiture, painting, art."

--T. NICHOLAS DAWIDOFF, "In a Whole Different League Now"

The Birth of Venus *by Botticelli, Uffizi, Florence*
Alinari/Art Resource

In the raising of a visor, and all it means, we may see things invisible to mortal sight in revelations of the human face divine shining through, purging and dispersing, the clouds. For Spenser the discovery of that divine face made human represents the evanescent moment to which he constantly returns, as he tries to seize the moment through language and thus reform the deformations wrought by Time and chance and change. Like Prince Arthur, his Roland, his Aeneas, Spenser strives to find a way to make the vision real; for, like his hero, Spenser wants to raise the final visor, lay aside the final dim veil, finally discover the face he worshiped most, the true and abiding face of his Queen, and of her green and pleasant land.

--A. BARTLETT GIAMATTI, *Exile and Change in Renaissance Literature* (Yale University Press © 1984 by Yale University)

EGGHEAD AT THE PLATE

Some Yale alums still cluck over the spectacle of Giamatti's descent from academic grandeur to the commercial muck of professional sports. If there is a life for former Ivy League presidents, it should be conducted as unobtrusively as possible in a reputable embassy or blue-chip foundation. At the other extreme, certain tobacco-chewing, spit-on-the-hands, belly-up-to-the bar baseball types wonder what in the hell a gabby professor is doing running a league and, next year, the whole show. Oh, yeah, Giamatti. Whattid he ever hit?

Yet when Bart explains the logic behind his errant pilgrimage, it all apparently makes sense. "Leaving the faculty at Yale in 1978 to become an administrator was the major transition," he says. "Every teacher who has ever been induced to defect to the other side invariably says"--he pounds the desk in mock emphasis--" 'I'm Going. To. Go. On. Teaching. By. Gosh.' It is psychologically necessary for them to say that. I said it. But it's never realistic. What I hope I became at Yale was a facilitator of those who are very, very good at what they do. That's also been my aim at the National League. It's what I'll try to do as commissioner."

--PAUL GRAY, "Egghead at the Plate"

"Some friends--I realized that I knew a lot of baseball fans on the faculty--even said, 'Great! Good for you!' For these valiant few I'd worked up a line that went, 'I'm almost fifty years old and I've just fallen in love and run away with a beautiful redhead with flashing eyes whose name is baseball.' "

--A. BARTLETT GIAMATTI, *from* "Celebration" *by* Roger Angell, *The New Yorker*

What was most noteworthy about him was that he continued to miss the pleasures of scholarly life, including, as he once described it, "that wonderful leisurely capacity, which was very intense, of going to the library with a problem and beginning to track it down, to hunt it, stalk it wherever it took you and then go grab it."

- -EDWARD B. FISK, "Baseball and Literature: Spiritual Cousins"

Come to think of it, the number of people on the Faculty of Arts and Sciences at Yale and the number of ballplayers in the major leagues are almost the same--somewhere around six hundred and thirty. And if we're making analogies, the umpires would be the deans. And tenure? Well, I guess even Mike Schmidt doesn't have tenure. Put the two bodies together, and what you have is one vast, unstable company of prima donnas. Skilled, yes, but oh, brother!

--A. BARTLETT GIAMATTI, *from* "Celebration" *by* Roger Angell, *The New Yorker*

BASEBALL'S RENAISSANCE MAN

" 'Controversy is baseball's milk,' said the game's new head dairyman."

"Last fall after the World Series," Giamatti says, "because there was a demonstrable difference between the two leagues and their interpretation of the balk rule in that portion which has to do with the set position"--he stands up now, in the middle of his league office, in the middle of his typically vast sentences, and starts into a pitcher's motion, his hands flying up together and then coming to rest on his pronounced paunch—"because the American League interpreted a change of direction as implicitly being a stop, and the National League interpreted a stop as an absence of motion, and because you had divergent interpretations and therefore divergence in balk calls, the rules committee met. Now who's on the rules committee?"

Giamatti goes down the list: three representatives from the National League, himself included; three from the American League, including Bobby Brown; three members of the National Association of Professional Baseball Leagues; representatives from the commissioner's office and from the umpires.

"All together there are about a dozen people," he continues. "Everybody in the room, with the exception of myself, has spent his life in major league baseball. We agreed quickly that the intention of the rule was that the hands had to come to a stop, you had to see a discernible stop, which was the National League's interpretation. It took no debate and it wasn't the league president's idea, this alien who never hit a major league fastball, Mr. Law and Order."

Giamatti goes on to talk about the new strike zone--a long, knowledgeable discourse on why the zone seemed to be dropping over the years and on the possible ways to readjust it in order to reclaim baseball's high strike. "The strike zone," he says, "that's where the conversation got long and interesting, all these baseball people standing up trying to figure out just where the armpits are exactly, even though no umpire was calling strikes there anymore. Then, because some people thought the American public was not ready to hear on television 'the nipple zone,' we decided to define the strike zone as the middle of the chest.

Bobby Brown. AP/Wide World

"Dr. Brown was marvelous. Every time someone would propose an anatomically inoffensive term, like the breastbone, he'd explain that wasn't where we wanted the strike zone to be. So we ended up with 'mid-chest to the knees,' first to avoid the specious argument about where armpits are and, second, by lowering the strike zone we hoped, in a paradox that ought not be beyond everyone's capacity to reason, to get umpires to focus on the high pitch more. That's all. All through spring training everyone was running around asking about the strike zone. Is it changed? Is it high? Is it low? Is it mine? Is it yours? So we all assumed that when the season began the big controversy would be the strike zone. Then the season opens. No one says a thing about the strike zone. No one says anything about ejecting players for throwing at batters. Balks!"

--CHARLES SIEBERT, "Baseball's Renaissance Man"

In truth, he has never abandoned teaching; he has moved his impressive pedagogical skills from the classroom into progressively larger arenas. Bart holds certain truths to be self-evident. Chief among these is his unfashionable conviction that individualism must cease when it threatens the legitimate, shared concerns of the community. This belief is not a late-blooming flower of incipient dotage. As a fledgling professor during the 1960s, Giamatti bore the plumage of the counterculture. His clothes were rumpled, his hair longish; he sported a goatee and an unassuming, downscale, fist-around- a-can-of-beer manner. Students were attracted by this charisma. They enrolled in his courses and came out of them equally entranced by their teacher, but for radically different reasons. Bart expected them to actually read their assignments. He believed in grades, tough grades; he argued that being a civilized human being is not a matter of instinct but of unrelenting hard work and discipline.

Nothing has changed, except that the stewardship of the national pastime has just been handed to a person who holds and acts upon deep moral convictions. He will be worth watching in the year ahead, as he attempts to protect his vision of the green, Edenic pageant against the clamoring demands of diverse actors, producers, stagehands and unruly spectators. Bart thinks he has an older, better idea: orderly, considerate crowds in clean, pleasant surroundings, absorbed in a leisurely spectacle performed by happy, fulfilled heroes.

--PAUL GRAY, "Egghead at the Plate"

Bust of Virgil, *Capitoline Museum, Rome Alinari/Art Resource*

VIRGIL'S GARDEN

They came to a land of joy,
 the green pleasaunces and
happy seats of the Blissful Groves.

"I worked as hard on my response to the Kevin Gross appeal as I worked on anything I did while I was in New Haven. It was challenging to try to be clear about cheating and what it meant, and to be fair at the same time."

Kevin Gross, a pitcher with the Phillies, was ejected from a game . . . and subsequently suspended for ten days, for affixing sandpaper to his glove, presumably in order to scuff the ball and alter its flight. Later on, I looked up the Giamatti opinion on the Gross appeal. Its ten pages of resonant text shone forth like Cardozo: "Acts of cheating are . . . secretive, covert acts that strike at and seek to undermine the basic foundation of any contest declaring the winner-- that all participants play under identical rules and conditions. They destroy faith in the game's integrity and fairness; if participants and spectators alike cannot assume integrity and fairness, and proceed from there, the contest cannot in its essence exist."

--ROGER ANGELL, "Celebration," *The New Yorker*

Parnassus *by Raphael, Vatican Alinari/Art Resource*

PINDAR'S PARADISE

Never the Muse is absent from their ways; lyres clash, and the flutes cry,
 and everywhere maiden choruses whirling.
They bind their hair in golden laurel and take their holiday.

Neither disease nor bitter old age is mixed in their sacred blood;
far from labor and battle they live. They escape scandal and litigation.

It breaks my heart because it was meant to, because it was meant to foster in me again the illusion that there was something abiding, some pattern and some impulse that could come together to make a reality that would resist the corrosion; and because after it had fostered again that most hungered for illusion, the game was meant to stop, and betray precisely what it promised.

--A. BARTLETT GIAMATTI, "The Green Fields of the Mind"

It is to his credit that Mr. Giamatti's insider's view hasn't changed his basic thinking on the labor issue. He declares that another baseball strike would be "a misfortune for everyone, not just the owners and players." He adds: "It would damage the people's trust in their institutions and the ability of groups in the public eye to surmount narrow self-interest." Also, he notes with almost-equal gravity, another fractured season would screw up the game's stats.

Yet he continues that his three years as National League prexy have taught him that Jovian pronouncements won't ensure baseball peace. "My influence will be what I make it, and I can't say for sure what that will be," he says quietly. "My charge is to preserve the integrity of the game. That's the basis for the prosperity of all the actors, you know, and if both sides keep it in mind it should help them work things out."

--FREDERICK C. KLEIN, "The Sultan of Swat"

I kid him that now his two major contributions to the world are the plumbing at Yale and inventing a new rule for baseball. You get fined if you "advance menacingly" toward another ballplayer. He's introduced the idea of advancing menacingly. I love it. It's such an English professor's ruling.

--JAMES V. MIROLLO, Professor of Renaissance Literature, Columbia University, from "Baseball's Renaissance Man" by Charles Siebert

He obviously loved the game, and baseball was in great hands with him as commissioner. I was looking forward to working with him. I liked and admired him. I will miss him and baseball will miss him.

—BILL WHITE, president of the National League, *The New York Time*

Commissioner of Baseball

Let it also be clear that no individual is superior to the game.
- -A. BARTLETT GIAMATTI, *from* the Commissioner's Statement

But then, like one of the great knights of *The Faerie Queene*, he was uprooted from the faculty, sent off to the presidency and the commissionership. On his 40th birthday, he was on a plane, going somewhere to raise money for Yale; on his 50th, a year ago, he was watching a ballgame with the Reds owner Marge Schott in Cincinnati. Now, just days after his 51st birthday, he is presiding over the National Pastime. *Nosce teipsum*, brave Giamatti. In the effort to get back home again, he has reached second base, with a good lead. His beard is white now, but it's April again, the parks smell like paradise, and his world is green.

- - FRANK DEFORD, "A Gentleman and a Scholar"

In baseball, the journey begins at home, negotiates the twists and turns at first and often founders far out at the edges of the ordered world at rocky second--the farthest point from home ...

- -A. BARTLETT GIAMATTI, *Take Time for Paradise*

As I think back and look forward, I see how nothing is straightforward, nothing is unambiguous; nothing I can see is without risk, is unmixed. Salvation does not come through simplicities, either of sentiment or of system. The gray, grainy complex nature of existence and the ragged edges of our lives as we actually lead them defy hunger for a neat, bordered existence and for spirits unsullied by doubt or despair.

-- A. BARTLETT GIAMATTI, *A Free and Ordered Space*

Remembering Bart's statement that "Being president of a university is no way for an adult to make a living," a reporter asked him:

"Sir, is being commissioner of baseball, likewise, any way for a grown-up to spend his waking hours?"

"Yes, an adult should be commissioner, because in any adult will always lurk a child, and if you don't try to find an adult for the job, the child will simply take over. You've got to watch that."

Will you then, sir, he was asked, issue a ... proclamation on the occasion of your ascent to the summit of the National Pastime?

"No, I tell myself, don't press it. Don't overdo it. This is a special world, baseball, and it certainly has its snakes in the garden, but I'm not sure that it needs a memo."

Also, baseball isn't about memos, thank God. It's about lineups, and should the new commissioner issue any such papal bull as he did during his tenure at Yale, it ought to be in the form of a lineup card, to be posted in hearts and dugouts everywhere. It should read:

HOME TEAM:

Green, CF

History, IB

Park, RF

Civility, 3B

Individual, 2B

Group, SS

Law, LF

Offense, C

Law, P

There would be no designated hitter.

--FRANK DEFORD, "A Gentleman and a Scholar"

ON THE DESIGNATED HITTER

The designated hitter is a very bad idea whose time is past. You extend the careers of some old hitters, but you're trading off younger pitchers who are being left in much too long, who are not pulled out for pinch hitters, who are not seasoned and often hurt themselves. They're simply left there.

You take away a lot of the strategy. And it violates a fundamental principle of a liberal education. This is a game where all nine guys are supposed to be able to play both games: offense and defense.

--A. BARTLETT GIAMATTI, *from* "Bart Giamatti Looks Ahead to National League Leadership" *by* David Corr

Last year, I watched a tape of a melee involving the Braves and the Reds, and I decided that Mr. Ozzie Virgil ... had played a less than useful role in it all, and I wrote him a letter to remonstrate with him. Well, Mr. Virgil, to his credit, picked up the phone and called me and said, "But you've got this exactly wrong. You misunderstood what you saw. I swung my arm like that because I was trying to get their guy off the pile." A few weeks after that, there was another mass misunderstanding, in another park, in which Mr. Virgil featured prominently as a peacemaker, and I called him and said I'd seen this, and that I appreciated it. After that, Mr. Virgil and I became more than nodding acquaintances, and that was nice.

--A. BARTLETT GIAMATTI, *from* "Celebration" *by* Roger Angell *The New Yorker*

Commissioner is a calling in a structure that has a secular religious calling. You're given extraordinary powers and faith, but you should only use them when it' really warranted.

--A. BARTLETT GIAMATTI, *from* "A Gentleman and a Scholar" *by* Frank Deford

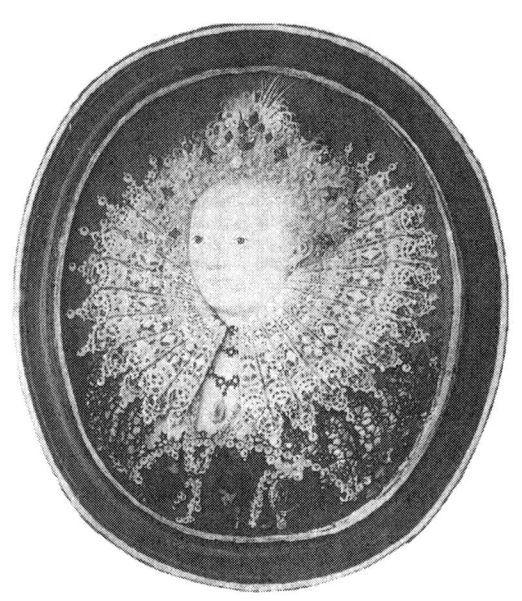

Miniature of Queen Elizabeth I by Nicholas Hilliard Victoria and Albert Museum, London. V & A /Art Resource

POWER

Elizabeth I was born on 7 September 1533 and ascended the throne on 17 November 1558. For the twenty-five years of her girlhood, adolescence, and young womanhood, she lived in the court of her father, Henry VIII, her brother, Edward VI, and her elder sister, Queen Mary. At court, by watching and waiting, she developed the instincts, the habits, and the style that later became her motto: *Taceo et video--I see and am silent.* Under Mary Tudor she learned how to give, as she would in the matter of Mary Stuart, "an answer answerless."

She learned she had no one to answer to if she was sufficiently self-possessed. She learned self-possession by watching the court and learning about power. Her innate powers of mind and character were developed so diligently that when she was sixteen Ascham could write a friend: "Her mind has no womanly weakness, her perseverance is equal to that of a man, and her memory long keeps what it quickly picks up." By watching, she also learned about public power. She learned that public power is a pure derivative of some overmastering idea about which all people agree; it is the force that accrues from some transcendent principle, the potency available for use in some bargain men make with heaven.

She learned that power derived from such an overarching idea can be held only if one becomes the embodiment of the idea oneself. Only by complete self-absorption can one contain the grand principle and the force that therefrom derives. She learned that to hold power she first had to deny herself--deny herself the ordinary delights of body and of spirit that otherwise disperse potency and principle. She early chose to deny herself those forms of dispersal represented by sex, by marriage and family, by the sense of wonder. She learned to deny herself that delicious, delightful human capacity to be smitten by anything outside of oneself. Wonder, a luxury she never tasted, would be for others, who adored and feared her.

- -A. BARTLETT GIAMATTI, "A Prince and Her Poet"

Pete Rose, *National Library, Cooperstown, New York*

THE COMMISSIONER'S STATEMENT

The banishment for life of Pete Rose from baseball is the sad end of a sorry episode. One of the game's greatest players has engaged in a variety of acts which have stained the game, and he must now live with the consequences of those acts. By choosing not to come to a hearing before me, and by choosing not to proffer any testimony or evidence contrary to the evidence and information contained in the report of the Special Counsel to the Commissioner, Mr. Rose has accepted baseball's ultimate sanction, lifetime ineligibility.

This sorry episode began last February when baseball received firm allegations that Mr. Rose bet on baseball games and on the Reds' games. Such grave charges could not and must never be ignored. Accordingly, I engaged and Mr. Ueberroth appointed John Dowd as Special Counsel to investigate these and other allegations that might arise and to pursue the truth wherever it took him. I believed then and believe now that such a process, whereby an experienced professional inquires on behalf of the Commissioner as the Commissioner's agent, is fair and appropriate. To pretend that serious charges of any kind can be responsibly examined by a Commissioner alone fails to recognize the necessity to bring professionalism and fairness to any examination and the complexity a private entity encounters when, without judicial or legal powers, it pursues allegations in the complex, real world.

Baseball had never before undertaken such a process because there had not been such grave allegations since the time of Landis. If one is responsible for protecting the integrity of the game of baseball--that is, the game's authenticity, honesty and coherence--then the process one uses to protect the integrity of baseball must itself embody that integrity. I sought by means of a Special Counsel of proven professionalism and integrity, who was obliged to keep the subject of the investigation and his representatives informed about key information, to create a mechanism whereby the integrity we sought to protect was never violated. Similarly, in writing to Mr. Rose on May 11, I designed, as is my responsibility, a set of procedures for a hearing that would have afforded him every opportunity to present statements or testimony of witnesses or any other evidence he saw fit to answer the information and evidence presented in the Report of the Special Counsel and its accompanying materials.

That Mr. Rose and his counsel chose to pursue a course in the courts rather than appear at hearings scheduled for May 25 an then June 26, and then chose to come forward with a stated desire to settle this matter, is now well known to all. My purpose in recounting the process and the procedures animating that process is to make two points that the American public deserves to know.

First, that the integrity of the game cannot be defended except by a process that itself embodies integrity and fairness.

Second, should any other occasion arise where charges are made or acts are said to be committed that are contrary to the interests of the game or that undermine the integrity of baseball I fully intend to use such a process and procedure to get to the truth and, if need be, to root out offending behavior. I intend to use, in short, every lawful and ethical means to defend and protect the game.

I say this so that there may be no doubt about where I stand or why I stand there. I believe baseball is a beautiful and exciting game, loved by millions--I among them--and I believe baseball is an important, enduring American institution. It must assert and aspire to the highest principles, of integrity, of professionalism of performance, of fair play within its rules. It will come as no surprise that like any institution composed of human beings, this institution will not always fulfill its highest aspirations. I know of no earthly institution that does. But this one, because it is so much a part of our history as a people and because it has such a purchase on our national soul, has an obligation to the people for whom it is played--to its fans and well-wishers--to strive for excellence in all things and to promote the highest ideals.

I will be told that I am an idealist. I hope so. I will continue to locate ideals I hold for myself and for my country in the national game as well as in other of our national institutions. And while there will be debate and dissent about this or that or another occurrence on or off the field, and while the game's nobler parts will always be enmeshed in the human frailties of those who, whatever their role, have stewardship of this game, let there be no doubt or dissent about our goals for baseball or our dedication to it. Nor about our vigilance and vigor-and patience-in protecting the game from blemish or stain or disgrace.

The matter of Mr. Rose is now closed. It will be debated and discussed. Let no one think that it did not hurt baseball. That hurt will pass, however, as the great glory of the game asserts itself and a resilient institution goes forward. Let it also be clear that no individual is superior to the game.

--A. BARTLETT GIAMATTI

The Earth *by Jan Breughel the Elder, Doria Gallery, Rome Alinari/Art Resource*

LOGISTILLA'S GARDEN

"It is only after we have read the poem *[Orlando Furioso]*, seen the peace of Logistilla's garden or the benign serenity of the true earthly paradise, that we begin to take the full measure of Alcina's garden. Dangerous and corrupting though it certainly was, false and deceptive though its illusions were, Alcina's garden remains as the image of a way of life which man can never wholly reject. He cannot reject it because it is so much a part of himself; it represented something reprehensible but profoundly enjoyable. Its danger lay not in what it did to you, but in what it allowed you to do to yourself. Though Alcina's paradise embodied a way of life which should be avoided, it also embodied something which can never be destroyed; and, therefore, no other garden virtuous or divine, in this poem devoted to the world, can ever replace it.

"Ariosto's gentle yet all-pervasive sense of the futility of human affairs must always be seen in relation to Alcina's garden. The garden teaches us that all deception is largely a matter of self-deception, and that no matter how strenuously we try to disagree, the final illusion is to think life would be at all bearable without illusions."

—A. BARTLETT GIAMATTI, *The Earthly Paradise and the Renaissance Epic*

I sort of lived with him [Giamatti] for six months on this case. He was one of the most precise human beings I have known and a man of extraordinary intellectual and verbal skill.

—JOHN DOWD, Investigator, Pete Rose case, *The New York Times*

I personally supported him in his bid to be commissioner. He was a brilliant man of supreme intellect. I felt he was going to be an outstanding commissioner. His handling of the Rose case certainly proved my theories I had going in. He was eminently fair, and I don't know anyone who had his passion for the game. A lot of guys love baseball, but he had a passion for it. He had as much integrity as anyone I've ever seen. When you combine that intellect with his integrity and passion, you have a rare individual.

- -FRANK CASHEN, former New York Mets General Manager, *The New York Times*

THE WORD "FUN"

Fun is, after all, the immediate purpose of the enterprise. It is necessary, however, if no fun, to remind ourselves that our word *fun* is probably derived from the obsolete verb *fun*, meaning *hoax* in the seventeenth century, itself probably a dialect variant of the obsolete *fun, to make a fool of*. After the word meant *hoax* (seventeenth century), it came to mean *sport* or *diversion* in the eighteenth century. When you are having fun, the English language believes, you are fooling yourself. "Sport" is based, here at least, on a practical joke, which is to say that sport is serious, but it is a trick, an illusion-- not real. That is the deepest way sport is conventional--it is a conscious agreement to enjoy, a pleasurable self-delusion. If sport aspires to contemplation, let us remember it begins in a con.

--A. BARTLETT GIAMATTI, *Take Time for Paradise*

I thought Giamatti had been fair with Rose. I thought it would have been fair to suspend Rose on Giamatti's first day on the job, April Fool's Day, when the first pile of evidence surfaced. I thought he had made mistakes, a mistake by waiting so long, a mistake by sending that letter to the federal judge, a mistake by giving Rose an out when the final ruling came down. Still, I thought he had been fair.

--MICHAEL MADDEN, "Tragic Case of Poetic Injustice"

David "Boo" Ferriss pitched the first game Bart saw in Fenway Park. *National Baseball Library, Cooperstown, New York*

Whether we see epic as emphasizing quest or exile, the impulse to go out and make cities, or to go home and rest; whether we stress the contradictory nature of fatherhood, or womanhood-in short, whether we opt for the specific focus of the *Iliad* or that of the *Odyssey* . .. we are taught that all human enterprise and endeavor involve a long, weary way. That to get there means going a long, long distance, a long space in time. We cannot escape epic's long view: that rest will come by never resting, that peace will come only by war, that all your future will be devoted, despite yourself and at best, to finding a memory from the past.

- -A. BARTLETT GIAMATTI, *Play of Double Senses: Spenser's* Faerie Queene

I think I've developed an agenda for baseball. I didn't come in with one. It seems the social issues are terribly important, the issues of affirmative action, expunging racism from baseball, issues of drugs and alcoholism are important, the issue of ambience at ballparks, and baseball's labor relations are not what they should be, that's got to be better in the sense of developing mutual respect and good feelings between the players association and major league baseball. I know that a league president or commissioner is often considered the creature of the owners, their craven shill, but I maintain the right to define myself as having a set of interests in mind, regardless of who hires me.

--A. BARTLETT GIAMATTI, *from* "Baseball's Renaissance Man" *by* Charles Siebert

He was a superb human being, a remarkable, intelligent, devoted father and husband, and a superb commissioner, as well as my dear friend.

--FAY T. VINCENT, former Commissioner of Baseball, *The New York Times*

In the Ballpark with Bart

Yes, yes, Dante is back out at the ballpark today.

--A. BARTLETT GIAMATTI, *from* "A Gentleman and a Scholar" *by* Frank Deford

Judge Kenesaw Mountain Landis, first Commissioner of Baseball. *National Baseball Library, Cooperstown, New York*

A FAN IN HIS OWN RIGHT

Baseball never was simply a matter of grace and courage and it is not now. It has had its share of mugs, but it has survived since the White Sox scandal of 1919 because the first duty of its commissioners has been to keep it as pure as humanly possible. An associate described Giamatti as fan-oriented, interested in seating and ballpark conditions and anything that would make watching and enjoying easier, not harder.

For a lot of us, the hardest part of winter is not snow or mudslides or water too cold for surfing but an absence of baseball, so being fan-oriented also means keeping the game clean. No matter how hard that was on Pete Rose and others whom Giamatti fined or suspended for cutting corners on the rules, that's what he was there for. In theory, a baseball game can go on forever. That has never happened, and nobody has a right even to expect extra innings in real life, but Giamatti's death last week at age 51 cut far too short the life of a scholar, a baseball fan and, in the most old-fashioned sense, custodian of what baseball means to a lot of Americans.

-- Editorial, *The Los Angeles Times*

Whether in a real city or not, when we enter that simulacrum of a city . . . the ballpark . . . and we have successfully, usually in a crowd, negotiated the thoroughfares of this special, set-aside city, past the portals, guarded by those who check our fitness and take the special token of admission, past the sellers of food, and vendors of programs, who make their markets and cry their news, and after we ascend the ramp or go through the tunnel and enter the inner core of the little city, we often are struck, at least I am, by the suddenness and fullness of the vision there presented: a green expanse, complete and coherent, shimmering, carefully tended, a garden.

-- A. BARTLETT GIAMATTI, *Take Time for Paradise*

There I was at the 1986 Red Sox-Mets World Series, sitting in the National League box! I'd told my son I planned to root for the Mets. He said he was confident I'd be able to rise above my duty. Sure enough, when things got close, an atavistic demon far more ancient than I took over. Before long I was advising Mr. Buckner (Bill, the ill-fated Red Sox first baseman) how to field his position, and Mr. MacNamara (John, the Sox's manager) what to do with his lineup.

Naturally, they paid me as much heed as they did any other nut.

--FREDERICK C. KLEIN, "The Sultan of Swat"

1986 World Series, Red Sox lose again. *National Baseball Library, Cooperstown, New York*

The first time I talked with him was at a spring training game between the Mets and Red Sox in St. Petersburg, Fla., in March 1987, the first game between the two since the World Series.

Giamatti said the rights, of how he was president of the National League and his natural passion for Boston, had to be curbed. But when Al Nipper plunked Darryl Strawberry in the first inning of that meaningless game, sparking a mini-rhubarb, I looked over to where Ueberroth and Giamatti were sitting. The commissioner had the proper and totally empty look on his face while watching this payback; Giamatti, the president of the league in which the Mets play, had a slight smile on his face. He was real.

--MICHAEL MADDEN, "Tragic Case of Poetic Injustice"

Tom Seaver, National baseball Library, Cooperstown

There was that muggy Sunday afternoon in late July when Giamatti and other dignitaries sat on folding chairs on the infield grass at Shea Stadium. The occasion was a love fest, the official retiring of the number (41) of the Mets former pitcher Tom Seaver. ... In the packed stands, goodwill and nostalgia outweighed even the humidity--until the public-address announcer, introducing the honored guests, reached Giamatti. "Boo!" the crowd responded. "Boooooooo!"

"All people in suits get booed at ballparks," Giamatti says .... "I was gratified by the response. I think it's healthy .... Remember what Seaver did at the end of the ceremony?" After a brief speech, the future Hall of Famer jogged to the pitching mound, the sphere of so many of his triumphs, and acknowledged wave after wave of ovations. "I'll tell you," Giamatti says, "that's one of my all-time baseball memories."

--PAUL GRAY. "Egghead at the Plate"

Scoreboard, Wrigley Field, Chicago. *National Baseball Library, Cooperstown, New York*

And whether there is, indoors or out, a wall or barrier separating spectator from player, whether bunting or music or mascots or marchers or leaping creatures in costume or advertising images gambol there, eventually the eye finds a device, hanging or looming, to tell the time and give the details and figure forth the score. This device knits up all the conventions, those the spectators (who make the city) bring, and those the players (who animate the garden) live with. It is a device whose refined capacities to reflect the action would be meaningless anywhere else in the wider or surrounding city. The scoreboard is the symbol of this garden-city's specialness. It tracks the negotiations that matter; it makes official whenever *negotium* achieves *otium*.

--A. BARTLETT GIAMATTI, *Take Time for Paradise*

1952 Boston Red Sox. *National Baseball Library, Cooperstown, New York*

Whether you see Fenway Park or Wrigley Field as an Eden or not, you are out there because you remember something that you want revived.

--A. BARTLETT GIAMATTI, *from* Baseball's Philosopher "King" *by* Ronald Schacter

Garden with Cascading Steps, Villa Frascati. *Alinari/Art Resource*

LIBANIUS' GARDEN

*Causes of delight are springs and plantations,
and gardens and soft breezes and flowers and bird-voices. . .*

THE FAN

Life: Has the fan changed?

Bart: In the last 20 years there has been increasing violence and rowdiness in the stands at all events. If there is a different kind of fan these days, he is a participatory fan who has been brought up on video images, which are meant to be interactive, a fan whose formative event was the rock concert. These are the people for whom the event is not something to sit and watch, but an excuse for other events--meeting friends, moving around, doing other things.

Life: But when people went to a game 40 years ago, wasn't it an interactive event?

Bart: Not the same way, because you went with friends, you didn't go to meet them. Less alcoholic beverages were consumed. The scoreboard was informational, it wasn't meant to stimulate you. And, finally, you didn't perceive reality by way of video imagery. Now you go to a game and you see people holding a little television set watching the game on the screen that is going on in front of them! I don't mean to be pejorative in my description of these new fans. It's just a wholly different attitude toward watching the game.

Life: So your task is to incorporate current realities with the basic of baseball.

Bart: Yes, and it's a fine line. I don't want the young thinking that baseball is some kind of stodgy event that is like church and I don't want older fans to think they can't come and enjoy the game because they'll be surrounded by people who are tumbling around and falling down flights of seats in a kind exuberant imitation of the energy that is being released on the field. And these issues seriously concern me: Technology will be so sophisticated in 10 years, the capacity to receive images will be so powerful, an aging society will be so disinclined to leave the house that the choice in 1995, I assume, will be whether to watch the soccer playoffs in Shanghai or a golf tournament in Kenya or the Phillies playing the Dodgers. We have to anticipate these new developments.

Life: Other institutions--the Broadway theater, the symphony orchestra--appear to be facing a similar quandary.

Bart: That's exactly right. I would put baseball in there with the museums and orchestras and the ballet companies and the regional theaters. All these institutions are rooted in history and instinctively think of history as part of what shaped them. And now they are all about to confront a world where a lot of people distrust institutions and where there is an instinctive American desire to think that you can start over every morning--a kind of Emersonian view that the dawn is coming and that what happens this morning is much better than anything that happened any morning before. That is both a source of tremendous strength and a historical view that is profoundly dangerous.

Life: What, then, are the essential elements of baseball?

Bart: It is a game that is exciting and stimulating and beautiful and fun, in part because it puts a tremendous premium on individual achievement in the context of a team. You're out there. And the ball comes to you at shortstop. There's nobody else who is going to pick it up for you, yet you're part of a team. I think Americans respond to that check and balance between the premium on the individual's talent and the overall team effort. I think that's part of the game's basic appeal: It is about boundary and rule and law, which we love in all phases of our life. Baseball is part of the fiber of American Life, and it must, by nature, appeal to and reflect the accessibility that is one of this society's great virtues. Classes and institutions are not closed off in a democracy and thus baseball must not be either.

Life: Any other essential elements?

Bart: That the sport doesn't change much. That it *is* traditional. Americans have become accustomed to associating summer's renewal of the earth and fall's harvest with baseball. You can't conceive of baseball being played in the winter. It is fitted to the season in an extraordinary way. There will be more domes, of course, and I'm not going to tell you that I don't lament that, but the notion of indoor baseball is being absorbed into our understanding of the game, like night baseball once had to be absorbed. This is how one incorporates the future while holding on to the essential.

Life: Certain changes, then, are acceptable.

Bart: As long as you don't tamper with baseball on the field, as long as you don't introduce, for instance, instant replay into umpiring and remove the whole principle of judgment and as long as you don't introduce limits on the allowable time between pitches. As long as you don't violate the game's fundamental trinitarian magic--the symmetry of three strikes, three outs, nine innings--as long as you don't change the field and the beauty of 90 feet--if it were 88 or 92 it would be a totally different game. As long as you don't do any of these things, baseball can adapt.
--TODD BREWSTER, "Front-office Fan"

On the field at Shea, Lenny Dykstra fouls three pitches into the crowd, then watches strike three and turns to glare at the umpire. Giamatti shifts in his seat, lights a cigarette and rubs his graying goatee. He repeats softly into his hand, "Go back to the dugout, Lenny. Go back to the dugout." Finally, Dykstra turns and walks off and Giamatti sighs. Another inning in paradise.

-- CHARLES SIEBERT, "Baseball's Renaissance Man"

On ballparks:

"More domes are coming, and I regret it. This game is meant to be played outdoors and on grass, but I don't see how we can expect a city to come up with a hundred-million dollar stadium-bond issue and not want to amortize that with conventions and car-crushing contests and football and the rest, which call for all-season stadiums. What I don't understand is the lack of imagination in ballpark design. ... Why can't we build an idiosyncratic, angular park, for a change, with all the amenities and conveniences, and still make it better than anything we have now? I just don't get it. A ballpark should be a box, not a saucer--everybody knows that-- but why couldn't we walk *down* to our seat for a change: dig a stadium, instead of always starting flat and then going up? It might even solve the wind problem in some places. Why can't we think up a stadium that would have some of the virtue of a Fenway Park--a place of weird angles and distances and beautiful ricochets? It could be done."

--A. BARTLETT GIAMATTI, *from* "Celebration" *by* Roger Angell, *The New Yorker*

Lefty Gomez. *National Baseball Library, Cooperstown, New York*

"I'm always interested when I go to spring training to sit and watch, in Florida or Arizona, older people: 60s, 70s, 80s," said Giamatti. "Looking at all of them. Watching them watch a baseball game. Watching them watch young men . . . . What do they see? They don't just see youngsters in relief. They see Vic Raschi, they see Lefty Gomez, some see Walter Johnson. You see history out there in every one of those young players because they all kind of pick up and remind you of a past you can't see anymore."

--PAUL D. BOWKER, "Baseball's Allure Eternal"

CELEBRATION

My wish to spend a couple of hours with Giamatti at the park came not from any desire to ferret out his views on the late news or the smoldering issues of the game or to quiz him about the commissionership . . . but from the prospect of listening to a lifetime .400 talker strut his stuff in the proper setting.

It was one of those moments when a game fulfills the home crowd's uttermost desires, and even after the teams had changed sides and we had stood and stretched and root-root-rooted for the home team, the party din continued to swell and beat all about us, as bits of paper and peanut shells took wing in the soft summer air. Giamatti stretched his arms along our seat backs and smiled and said, "Look, just look. Even the weather has changed-- it's a great night for baseball. Here's a big, beautiful crowd behaving itself and having the time of its life, and I'm the only guy here in a coat and tie. But I don't care-- you can't have everything, can you?

"Look," Giamatti went on, in his alert, cheerful way. "You and I are traditional fans. We come here in a ceremonial fashion. We don't exactly kneel, but we're interested only in that stuff"--he gestured at the diamond and the outspread field before us--"for our basic information. We come to testify. We're not participatory fans. For them, that object"--he pointed to the towering Diamond Vision board in left center--"is more important than anything that happens on the field. For them, it's the video and the dot races and the commercials which are probably all connected to rock music in the end. For us, it's still the pitcher and the batter and the score, which are connected to the printed page. This is our text, that's theirs ... . It's going to be interesting to see how baseball accommodates itself to these two audiences.

Lee Weyer. *National Baseball Library, Cooperstown, New York*

"Umpires are a brotherhood," Giamatti said .... "Lee Weyer never married, but he was a warm man. One thing I remember about him is the way he dusted off the plate. He'd dust it clean and then he'd make this clear outline around the perimeter of the plate, with his brush. Nobody else did that. ... "

I remembered, almost as an afterthought, that he was a writer, and over the next week or two I found some of his books and began to dip into them at odd moments, reading almost at random and looking more for the author than for some new appreciation of bygone prosody or passion. One day, leafing through "Exile and Change in Renaissance Literature," I thought I had a sudden glimpse of him--not with his tie and blazer but in brighter, heraldic colors--in the person of Matteo Boiardo, a fifteenth century Italian poet, whose great work was "Orlando Innamorato."

"Boiardo's deepest desire is to conserve something of purpose in a world of confusion," Giamatti had written. "He knows that chivalry is an outmoded system, but he wants to keep something of its value, its respect for grace and noble behavior, even while he relinquishes its forms and structures. . . . Boiardo wants to check the urge to dissolution…that time seems inevitably to embody. He does not want to turn back the clock and regain the old world, but he does want to recapture the sense of control of oneself, if nothing else, that marked life under the old system. He wants to be able to praise something other than the giddy, headlong rush."

--ROGER ANGELL, "Celebration," *The New Yorker*

Maybe I love baseball so much because I wasn't very good at it. Anyway, my coach used to send me behind the backstop during games to check on the umpires, so I began watching umpires at a very early age.

--A. BARTLETT GIAMATTI *from* "Baseball's Renaissance Man" *by* Charles Siebert

On inside pitches:

"The umpire is caught in the middle--as usual. Because of some recent changes, he has to issue warnings from time to time, not because he thinks anything is going on but only because the batter is upset. It's a general warning--to keep order, but not as a result of any infraction or intention. And that's too bad: it's a misuse. The batters have the upper hand just now, and they're much less inclined to put up with something that was once accepted as a normal part of the game."

--A. BARTLETT GIAMATTI *from*" Celebration" *by* Roger Angell, *The New Yorker*

The pride in umpiring has really come forward in the last couple of years. I couldn't say enough about Bart Giamatti, and not because he's a friend, not because we signed a good deal. That has nothing to do with it. The guy has *time* for us. We've got a working relationship we've never had before. I've got an interview with him on my desk now. He's talking about complaints he hears about the umpires. "Hey," he says, "I love the umpires."

--BRUCE FROEMMING, major league umpire. Mike Bryan, "Baseball Lives"

A Shape So Gay

And often toward the heavens he raised his head

Whereto the gentle soul had made ascent

Which had been mistress of a shape so gay.

--DANTE ALIGHIERI, "A New Life"

Baseball card of A. Bartlett Giamatti. *Leaf, Inc.*

A. Bartlett Giamatti was to the Commissioner's office what Sandy Koufax was to the pitcher's mound: Giamatti's career had the highest ratio of excellence to longevity. If his heart had been as healthy as his soul--if his heart had been as strong as it was warm-- Giamatti would one day have been ranked among commissioners the way Walter Johnson is ranked (by correct thinkers) among the pitchers: as the best, period.

--GEORGE F. WILL, *Men at Work*

Former Baseball Commissioner Fay T. Vincent.
Harry Benson

THE COMMISSIONER'S PINCH HITTER

On the surface, they seemed an odd pair—Giamatti, the witty Renaissance scholar and former president of Yale, and Vincent, the reserved lawyer and former chairman and CEO of Columbia Pictures Industries Inc. They were introduced at the Princeton home of a mutual friend a dozen years ago. "We were friends from the moment we met," says Vincent. It turned out they shared both their ages and Yale--Giamatti attended as an undergraduate, Vincent as a law student. "Bart said to me that night, 'Whose job is better?' He was president of Yale, and I was head of Columbia Pictures, and we agreed they were both impossible jobs. Then I said my job was better, and he asked me why, and I pointed out that I made $300,000, about three times what he earned. He laughed. He had a great capacity for joy, great energy." In the years that followed, says Vincent, "We often talked about working together. Bart said that whatever we do, we should do it together. If he had a job where he could hire me, he would, and if I had a job where I could hire him, I would. But the important thing was that we would be together."

When Vincent became executive vice president of the Coca-Cola Company in 1986, he tried to find a job for Giamatti. "But there was nothing for him there," he says. Still, they kept up.

Vincent gave up his high-paying job at Coca-Cola to work for his friend as baseball's first deputy commissioner. Much of their energy was spent on the Pete Rose case, but this did not stop them from getting out to the ballpark on a regular basis. "We went to Yankee Stadium," recalls Vincent, "and the fans all knew Bart and teased him, and he teased them back. He wouldn't sit in the press box; he sat among the fans. That's where he wanted to be."

--KEN GROSS, "The Commissioner's Pinch Hitter"

How do you design something for a classics scholar (I know nothing about classics) and a family man Italian in origin who taught on a Gothic campus?

I began to think of the simplest of things, the notion of conversation, one of Bart's prize values--the notion of one human being exchanging something with another. I thought of the great monasteries, which were the forerunners of the campus. In the great monasteries, information was communicated in the oral tradition, from person to person. They walked in an infinite path, as if infinity really is a sense of conversation, and communication came from walking a rectangular path in a courtyard.

— —DAVID SELLERS, designer of the bench at Yale memorializing Bart Giamatti

I'm absolutely shattered. He was a very good friend. He was perhaps the finest commissioner baseball ever had.

— — AL ROSEN, Giants general manager, *The New York Times*

GIAMATTI'S GRAND ODYSSEY

It was the time of Timothy Leary, Bobby Seales, Cesar Chavez, Cambodia, Vietnam, ROTC.

It was the time of the Apollo moon landing, Woodstock.

It was then that I first met Bart Giamatti. He was the university's youngest college master, a sort of academic and social mentor to more than

300 undergraduates who lived together in one of Yale's residential colleges.

He knew us by name. He knew where most of us were from. He made us feel we belonged at a time when we felt apart from our teachers, our parents, ourselves. He could find in the twenty-five-hundred-year-old works of Homer a safe mooring for the sojourner of 1969.

I remember the May 8, 1973, farewell address he gave to us hundred-odd seniors. There was a somber quality to that night. For some of us, Vietnam waited; for more, grad school; for all, a deep and abiding skepticism about the future of our nation, our world, ourselves.

"Let us look back to the beginning of things and there maybe find our proper ending," he said, likening us to a modern-day Odysseus who must endure toil and trouble before returning home to any safe haven. "And when you get on land, think of us still at sea.

"You've had a grand cruise," he said.

Indeed, Bart, so have you. And we pray that somewhere is a quiet harbor for us all.

--BOB UNGER, editor, *Holyoke Transcript-Telegram*

His major message, as I saw it, was that the artist's purpose in the epic was to put the reader through the same soul-searching regimen as the epic hero in his quest for earthly perfection. To understand *The Divine Comedy* we slogged through the Slough of Despond, climbed the rings of Purgatory and burst into the Empyrean, Bart at the lead, lighting the way, making sense of Dante's classical and historic allusions as a sport

fanatic cites stats and recalls historic moments,
living their lessons.

—W. DEWOLF FULTON, "A. Bartlett Giamatti; Retrospective of a Role Model"

Singers by *Luca della Robia, Museo dell'Opera del Duomo, Florence. Alinari/Art Resource*

DANTE'S WORDS OF GRIEF

For ever, among all my sighs which burn,
There is a piteous speech
That clamours upon Death continually:
Yea, unto him doth my whole spirit turn

Since first his hand did reach My lady's life with most foul cruelty.
But from the height of woman's fairness, she,
Going up from us with the joy we had,
Grew perfectly and spiritually fair;
That so she spreads even there
A light of Love which makes the Angels glad,
And even unto their subtle minds can bring
A certain awe of profound marvelling.

- -DANTE ALIGHIERI, *A New Life*

A. Bartlett Giamatti. *National Baseball Library, Cooperstown*

For all the knowledge that we will never succeed in the work of our lives, we must continue to choose to continue. For all the frustration and fears that each of us has and will have in our short time, we must choose to pursue to the end of choosing the best we know for ourselves and for each other, and in that choosing, long and late, we will connect with each other.

--A. BARTLETT GIAMATTI, *A Free and Ordered Space New York*

BART'S GARDEN

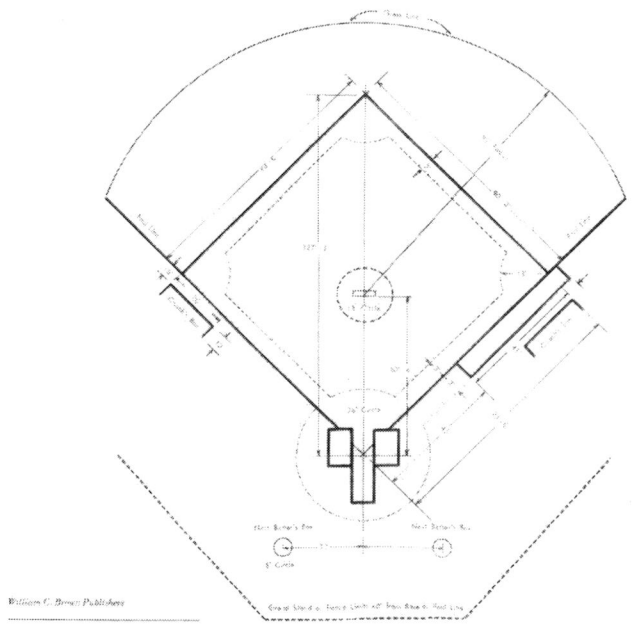

William C. Brown Publishers

Acknowledgments

SPECIAL THANKS

This book was inspired by the life, work, and vision of A. Bartlett Giamatti. After him come the ballplayers and the poets. Hats off to my visionary GM and field manager Ellen Nerenberg who gives me the hit sign on 3 and 0 counts. Of the many people who made this book a reality, Robert Brower is among the first. His understanding was profound, his belief grand and pure, and he worked hard during every phase. After his pilgrimage to the archives of Mount Holyoke, Robert wrote: "I fell in love with Valentine Giamatti. He symbolizes for me the heart link, the protector of the spirit." Robert

Brower protected the spirit of this book. If any of our hearts have linked with Bart's, it is to Robert Brower that we owe immense gratitude. Through his great technical know-how, good friend and valued colleague C-J Caesar made this edition possible. Bill Valerio guided me through the Renaissance Gardens. In the Caffe Dante, Shel Silverstein stimulated me to do it and gave me the title. Bonnie Brower guided the book to the wonderful Frances Goldin who then ushered it to Cork Smith who took it in with compassion and elegance. Our special thanks.

CURATORIAL ACKNOWLEDGMENTS

For their cooperation and patience, we would like to thank the librarians and archivists who took part, especially Dan Bennett and Patricia

Kelly at the National Baseball Library, Cooperstown, New York; Gerhard Gruitrooy at Art Resource; Phyllis Collazo at the *New York Times;* Anne C. Edmonds and Elaine D. Trehab of Mount Holyoke College Library; and Connie Clancy of the South Hadley Library System.

The following works are reproduced courtesy of Alinari/Art Resource:

Allegory of Spring by Botticelli; Uffizi, Florence. *The Birth of Venus* by Botticelli; Uffizi, Florence. *Cantoria* by Lucca della Robbia; Museum of the Duomo, Florence. *Portrait of Dante,* Anonymous; National Museum, Florence. *The Earth* by Jan Brueghel; Doria Gallery, Rome. *Expulsion* by Masaccio; Brancacci Chapel, Florence. *Bust of*

Homer, Rome, Capitoline Museum. *Bust of Virgil*, Anonymous; Capitoline Museum, Rome. *Hercules and the Centaur* by Giovanni Bologna; Loggia dei Lanzi, Florence. Illustration of *Orlando Furioso* by Sebastiano Ricci; Museo Brukenthal, Romania. *Palazzo Pitti and Belvedere* by van Utens, Museum of Florence. *Parnassus* by Raphael; Vatican. *Poetry* by Raphael; Vatican. *Renaissance Garden of the Villa Medici at Pratolino* by van Utens; Museum of Florence. *Villa Frascati, with Cascading Steps*; Alinari/Art Resource.

The following works are reproduced courtesy of Giraudon/Art Resource:

The Barbieri Races by Gericault; Louvre, Paris. Illustrations by Botticelli for *The Divine Comedy*; National Library, Paris. *Jupiter and Thetis* by Ingres;

Musée Granet, Aix en Provence. *Paradise* by Jan Brueghel; Musée des Beaux-Arts, Besançon. *Don Quichotte* by Daumier is reproduced courtesy SEF/Art Resource. The miniature of Elizabeth I by Hilliard is reproduced courtesy of the Victoria and Albert Museum, London, and Art Resource.

PERMISSIONS

Our appreciation and gratitude go out to the Estate of A. Bartlett Giamatti, to Mrs. Toni Giamatti, to Mrs. Valentine Giamatti, and to Mildred Marmur. Bansie Vasvani persevered in gaining permissions. Thanks to the publishers, authors, editors, and translators for permission to reprint the following: A. Bartlett Giamatti baseball card. Reprinted by permission of Leaf.

Inc. Excerpts from "A. Bartlett Giamatti; Retrospective of a Role Model" by W. Dewolf Fulton. Reprinted by permission of the author. "Bart's Garden" from *The Complete Baseball Handbook: Strategies and Techniques for Winning*, second edition, by Walter Alston and Don Weiskopf. Copyright © 1989 by William C. Brown Publishers. All rights reserved. Reprinted by permission of William C. Brown Publishers, Dubuque, Iowa. Excerpt from "Bart Giamatti Looks Ahead to National League Leadership" by David Corr. Copyright © 1986 by Vineyard Gazette Inc. Reprinted by permission. Excerpt from "Baseball's Allure Eternal" by Paul D. Bowker. Copyright © *The TranscriptTelegram*, Holyoke, MA. Reprinted by permission. Excerpt from "Baseball and the American Character," a speech to the Massachusetts Historical Society, by A. Bartlett Giamatti. Copyright © by A. Bartlett Giamatti. Reprinted by permission. Excerpt from "Baseball Commissioner Giamatti Dies--Red Sox Lose a Friend of Their Family" by Frank Dell'Apa. Copyright © 1989 by *The Boston Globe*. Reprinted by permission. Excerpts from "Baseball and Literature: Spiritual Cousins" by Edward B. Fiske. Copyright © 1989 by The New York Times Company. Reprinted by permission. Excerpt from *Baseball Lives* by Mike Bryan. Copyright © 1989 by Mike Bryan. Reprinted by permission of Bruce Froemming. Excerpt from "Baseball's Philosopher King" by Ronald Schacter. Copyright © by Ronald Schacter. Reprinted by permission. Excerpts from "Baseball's Renaissance Man" by Charles

Siebert. Copyright © 1988 by The New York Times Company. Reprinted by permission. Excerpt from "The Commissioner's Pinch Hitter" by Ken *Gross/People* Weekly. Copyright © 1989 by Time Inc. Magazines. Reprinted by permission. Excerpt from "Dante to Doerr" by Nick Johnson. Copyright © by *The Transcript-Telegram*, Holyoke, MA. Reprinted by permission. Ron Darling photo reprinted by permission of Photo File. Excerpts from "A Desire to Excel" by Frank Deford. Reprinted courtesy of *Sports Illustrated* from the 3/30/81 issue. Copyright © 1981, Time, Inc. All rights reserved. Joe DiMaggio photo reprinted courtesy of *The Sporting News*. Excerpts from *The Earthly Paradise and the Renaissance Epic* by A. Bartlett Giamatti.

Reprinted by permission of The Estate of A. Bartlett Giamatti and Mildred Marmur Associates Ltd. Excerpts from "Egghead at the Plate" by Paul Gray. Copyright © 1988 by Time-Warner Inc. Reprinted by permission. Excerpts from *Exile and Change in Renaissance Literature* by A. Bartlett Giamatti. Copyright © 1984 by Yale University. All rights reserved. Reprinted by permission of Yale University Press. Excerpt from "A Fan in His Own Right" by Los Angeles Times Editorial. Copyright © 1989 by *The Los Angeles Times*. Reprinted by permission. "Fishing with Bart" by Robert Brower. Courtesy of the author. Excerpts from *A Free and Ordered Space: The Real World of the University* by A. Bartlett Giamatti. Reprinted with the permission of W. W. Norton & Company, Inc.

Copyright © 1988, 1987, 1986, 1985, 1984, 1983, 1982, 1981, 1980, 1979, 1978, 1976 by A. Bartlett Giamatti. Excerpts from "Front-office Fan: Interview with A. Bartlett Giamatti" by Todd Brewster. Copyright © 1988 by Time Warner Inc. Reprinted from *Life* Magazine by permission. Excerpts from "A Gentleman and a Scholar" by Frank Deford. Reprinted courtesy of *Sports Illustrated* from the 4/17/89 issue. Copyright © 1989, The Time, Inc. Magazine Company. All rights reserved. Excerpts from "Giamatti a Simple Lover of Baseball" by Kevin Paul Dupont. Copyright © 1989 by *The Boston Globe*. Reprinted by permission. Excerpt from "Giamatti's Grand Odyssey" by Bob Unger. Reprinted by permission of the author. Excerpts from "Giamatti, Scholar and Baseball Chief, Dies at 51" by Robert D. McFadden. Copyright © 1989 by The New York Times Company. Reprinted by permission. Excerpts from "The Green Fields of the Mind" by A. Bartlett Giamatti. Reprinted by permission of The Estate of A. Bartlett Giamatti and Mildred Marmur Associates Ltd. Excerpts from "He Had a Great Passion" by Judy Van Handle. Copyright © 1989 by *The Boston Globe*. Reprinted by permission. Excerpts from "He'll Be Forever Linked with Sox" by Jack Craig Copyright © 1989 by *The Boston Globe*. Reprinted by permission. Holiday card photo by Thomas Jacob. Reprinted by permission of Mr. Jacob. Excerpt from "Hometown Stunned, Saddened" by Judy Van Handle Copyright © 1989 by *The Boston Globe*. Reprinted by permission. "Horace's

Paradise" from *The Odes and Episodes* translated by C. E. Bennett. Copyright © 1946 by Harvard University Press. Reprinted by permission from Harvard University Press. Excerpts from "In a Whole Different League Now" by T. Nicholas Dawidoff. Reprinted courtesy of *Sports Illustrated* from the 10/27/86 issue. Copyright © 1986, Time, Inc. All rights reserved. Excerpts from "Insight" by Cynthia Mann. Copyright © 1985 by *The Transcript-Telegram*, Holyoke, MA. Reprinted by permission. Excerpts from "Lessons" by Edward B. Fiske. Copyright © 1989 by The New York Times Company. Reprinted by permission. Excerpt from "Like Many, He Found Peace on the Island" by Ron Borges. Copyright © 1989 by *The Boston Globe*. Reprinted by permission. Excerpt from *Men at*

Work by George F. Will. Copyright © 1989 by George F. Will. Reprinted by permission of Macmillan Publishing Company. Excerpts from *A New Life* by Dante Alighieri, translated by D. G. Rossetti. Reprinted by permission of Penguin USA. Excerpts from *The Odyssey* by Homer, translated by Robert Fitzgerald. Copyright © 1961, 1963 by Robert Fitzgerald, renewed 1989 by Benedict R. C. Fitzgerald. Reprinted by permission of Vintage Books, a Division of Random House, Inc. Excerpts from "Peers Reflect on the Loss of Giamatti" by Joe Sexton. Copyright © 1989 by The New York Times Company. Reprinted by permission. "Pindar's Paradise" from *The Odes of Pindar* by Pindar, translated by R. Lattimore. Chicago, 1947. Excerpts from *Play of Double Senses: Spenser's* Faerie

Queene, by A. Bartlett Giamatti. Reprinted by permission of The Estate of A. Bartlett Giamatti and Mildred Marmur Associates Ltd. Excerpt from "A Prince and Her Poet" by A. Bartlett Giamatti. Copyright © 1984 by the *Yale Review*. Reprinted by permission. Excerpt from "Professor Giamatti Retires from Mount Holyoke College." Copyright © 1973 by Vineyard Gazette Inc. Reprinted by permission. Excerpt from "Professor Hardball" by Brenton Welling and William C. Symonds. Copyright © 1989 by *Business Week* Magazine. Reprinted by permission. Professor Valentine Giamatti photo lent by Mrs. Valentine Giamatti. Reprinted by permission of Mount Holyoke College Library/Archives. Quote by Dick Schaap, courtesy of Mr. Schaap. Excerpts from "The Sporting Scene:

Celebration" by Roger Angell. Copyright © 1988 by Roger Angell. All rights reserved. Reprinted from *The New Yorker* by special permission. South Hadley Bicentennial Parade photo reprinted by permission of South Hadley Library System, Connie Clancy, Director. Excerpts from "The Sultan of Swat" by Frederick C. Klein. Copyright © *The Wall Street Journal.* Reprinted by permission. Excerpts from *Take Time for Paradise: Americans and Their Games* by A. Bartlett Giamatti. Copyright © 1989 by the Estate of A. Bartlett Giamatti. Reprinted by permission of Summit Books, a division of Simon & Schuster, Inc. "Theocritus' Garden" from *The Greek Bucolic Poets,* translated by J. E. Edmonds. Copyright © 1935 by Harvard University Press. Reprinted by permission of

Harvard University Press. "Tom Seaver's Farewell: There Is No Joy in Gotham" by A. Bartlett Giamatti. Reprinted by permission of The Estate of A. Bartlett Giamatti and Mildred Marmur Associates Ltd. Excerpts from "Tragic Case of Poetic Injustice" by Michael Madden. Copyright © 1989 by *The Boston Globe*. Reprinted by permission. "Virgil's Garden" from *Virgil*, translated by H. R. Fairclough. Copyright © 1935 by Harvard University Press. Reprinted by permisson of Harvard University Press. Quote by Professor Paolo Valesio, courtesy of Prof. Valesio. Excerpt from "Yale's MVP Learns New Signals-and Sends Some" by Edward B. Fiske. Copyright © 1979 by The New York Times Company. Reprinted by permission. Excerpt from "Yale's Renaissance Man" by

William Henry III. Copyright © 1978 by *The Boston Globe.* Reprinted by permission.

Hartsville Memorial Library
147 W. College Ave.
Hartsville, SC 29550
843-332-5115